GARNETT LIBRARY
SMSU-WEST PLAINS WITHDRAWN
SU-WP Garnett Library

PS
3543
.A563
Z62
1998

Discov
remin

D0734515

981200

| DATE | | | |
|------|--|--|--|
| *fac* | | | |
| | | | |
| | | | |
| | | | |
| | | | |
| | | | |
| | | | |
| | | | |
| | | | |
| | | | |
| | | | |

BAKER & TAYLOR

# Discovery *and* Reminiscence

# Discovery *and* Reminiscence

## Essays on the Poetry of Mona Van Duyn

Edited by Michael Burns

The University of Arkansas Press
Fayetteville ∞ 1998

Copyright 1998 by Michael Burns

All rights reserved
Manufactured in the United States of America

02  01  00  99  98    5  4  3  2  1

*Designed by Liz Lester*

⊛  The paper used in this publication meets the minimum requirements of the American National Standard for Permanence of Paper for Printed Library Materials Z39.48-1984.


*Library of Congress Cataloging-in-Publication Data*

Discovery and reminiscence : essays on the poetry of
    Mona Van Duyn / edited by Michael Burns.
          p.    cm.
      Includes bibliographical references (p.    ).
      ISBN 1-55728-473-3 (c.)
      1. Van Duyn, Mona—Criticism and interpretation.
    2. Women and literature—United States—History—
    20th century.   I. Burns, Michael, 1953–       .
    PS3543.A563Z62     1998
    811'.54—dc21                                    97-37474
                                                      CIP

Poems and passages from poems by Mona Van Duyn from her books *If It Be Not I: Collected Poems 1959–1982, Near Changes,* and *Firefall* are reprinted by permission of Alfred A. Knopf, Inc. "Matters of Poetry" is reprinted by permission of the author.

# Contents

# Contents

# Introduction

This book has a simple purpose: the thoughts collected here pay tribute to a great American poet, Mona Van Duyn, and they enlarge (and encourage) a discussion of the impressive body of her work. The contributors are themselves poets, and their critical responses to Van Duyn's poetry address not only its structure and theme but also its invaluable, lasting influence.

Maxine Kumin, Carolyn Kizer, and Richard Howard, having staked their own Pulitzer flags on the literary landscape, bring authority and a personal touch to the first section of the book. All three have long been supporters of Van Duyn's work. Kumin describes the poems' "quirkiness that deepens into exactitude," and Kizer points out that Van Duyn "shows that the ordinary is strange, with a strangeness that only an artist can reveal to us." Howard graciously chose to contribute a new poem to this collection, a warm and funny memoir that praises Van Duyn's poetry for "renouncing the possession of wisdom / in favor of the power to observe."

The contributors represented in part 2 have also established reputations in contemporary American letters as poet-critics. The essays by these writers show them making careful examinations of a poetry which exists for them as both example and inspiration. They teach us how to read, reminding us of what is especially worthy of praise. Stephen Yenser says that Van Duyn "is as responsible as any recent poet for bringing to our attention the deliquescent, catabolic, chaotic nature of things." Rachel Hadas says, "To read Van Duyn is less to marvel at how much she gets into her poems, so natural do they seem, than to be reminded how very much of life most poets leave out." And from Sidney Burris, "It is one of the important accomplishments of Van Duyn's work to remind us that in a free state the insouciance of one poet is no less essential than the gravity of another." Essays by these contributors describe specific themes in Van Duyn's poetry. Ann Townsend shows us how the poetry "avoids the elegiac impulse in favor of a poetic that allows the body, the survivor, to speak her own last words." Michael Bugeja, himself a professor of journalism as well as a poet, offers the poetry of Van Duyn as perhaps the best antidote to a society where the influence of mass media continues to cheapen our language. Any reader of Van Duyn's work will know that Leda has been a major figure in several poems. Wyatt Prunty discusses these poems and others as examples of the important theme of metamorphosis in Van Duyn's poetry, focusing also on her use of humor. Jane Hoogestraat completes the colloquy. Her essay talks about Van Duyn as a poet who faces cultural issues head on, describing her as someone who writes from "the center of American culture," whose poetry "bears the mark of gender difference."

Part 3 supplies readers with information they might logically seek in a collection of essays such as this one. Van Duyn's own opinions about the state of contemporary American poetry are presented in her essay "Matters of Poetry," an edited version of her poet laureate address to the Library of Congress. And those who want a careful, chronological presentation of the details of Van Duyn's literary and academic career will find it in Beth Snow's "Biographical Notes."

"Three Valentines to the Wide World," one of Van Duyn's early poems, speaks clearly about her lifelong commitment to poetry, and a phrase from it serves as the title for this collection. Perhaps a longer passage will serve best as both an introduction and a transition here:

    Only the poem
is strong enough to make the initial rupture,
at least for me. Its view is simultaneous
discovery and reminiscence. It starts with the creature

and stays there, assuming creation is worth the time
it takes, from the first day down to the last line on the last page.

# I ∞ Tributes

# Back to the Fairground

## Maxine Kumin

The other day I took Mona Van Duyn's *Near Changes* down from the shelf and gave myself over to the luxury of rereading these poems, underscored here and there in yellow marker from my first enthusiastic encounter with them in 1990. What I remarked on then was her warm affection for the things of her world—an infant giraffe, neighborhood dogs, the spectacular sunsets that followed the conflagrations in Yellowstone, the light cast by a Coleman lantern in a log cabin, the homely dailiness of long marriage. All these acquire a special patina on reacquaintance, surprising me again and again with an outspoken quirkiness that deepens into exactitude as I reread and reabsorb.

Consider the flat declarative statement that opens "Falling in Love at Sixty-Five": "It is like the first and last time I tried a Coleman / for reading in bed in Maine." "It?" The act of falling in love posited in the title and never further elucidated? Instead, in loving detail, we are given a narrative of the lantern itself, which becomes a fearsome, loved object, its "instant outcry roaring its threat to explode the walls." Further, "the lamp called out / the guilty years," it illuminated the book "in colors of lightning and thunder . . . in its artistry and rage." We are tricked into the plot of this poem, teased by parallel episodes of blue butterflies and night-flying moths, and brought back at the end to "the speaking light" of the lantern. I chewed a long time on the title and its purported relationship to the text. Is falling in love late in life as tyrannous and brightly illuminating as the extended simile of the Coleman lamp suggests? As passionate and obsessive as the creatures drawn to the lamp, "the blind wanting that stuffed full each carapace / in a clicking crash at the lampglass"?

Perhaps there's a hint in the poem immediately following, "Late Loving," where we learn "'Love' is finding the familiar dear. / 'In love' is to be taken by surprise."

Reading Van Duyn is to be taken by surprise, line by line. She speaks of living "in double rooms whose temperature's controlled / by matrimony's turned-down thermostat." No sooner have I adjusted to that domestic metaphor than I am caught by an equally felicitous, outwardly prosy, wonderfully apt one: "Squabbling onward, we chafe from being so near. / But all night long we lie like crescents of Velcro, / turning together till we re-adhere."

The charm of these two poems resides in the imagery. Van Duyn is able to take the oldest and potentially most boring of virtues, monogamy, and freshen it with lively and compelling figures.

When she turns her attention to a mundane event in the outside world, she brings to it that same sense of wonder, this time coupled with terror and release. "First Trip through the Automatic Carwash" charmed me all over again as I reexperienced my own infrequent voyages through Van Duyn's. From the opening unexpected question, "Clamped to another will, the self in its glass / begins a slow, tugged slide, toward what clarifying?" I, too, am tugged in a childlike trance of terror and delight. I go from "Drenching and blindness" to "a fierce forest whose long dark leaves wrap [me] in a wild / and waving threat."

The rhetorical question is a favorite device of this poet. Trapped, however voluntarily, inside the car as it is being cleaned, she asks, "What is whirling away? The long wedlock, / its bolt ground loose? Or the whole safe cage / of sane connections?" Indeed, these are the questions the entire book raises as the poet struggles, like E. M. Forster, "to forget the India of the chaotic heart." And who else, in a poem titled "The Ferris Wheel," could ask, "Does it remind you too / of the passionate climax, then the slow drift downward / into slums of sleep?"

Suspended in her chair in this same poem, Van Duyn sums up what has been her personal quest over a long and fully engaged life:

> Tell me how we can marry enthroned, imperious love
> to common human kindness, in order to live
> the only life worth living, the empathic life . . .
>
> (A last trip upward would be an anticlimax,
> the Wheel being too worldly to speak to everything.
> But if the stem should snap from a clumsy touch
> of Nature's overpowering tropes, let it be said
> that she counts on gravity to bring her back
> finally, and for good, to the fairground. . . .)

# A
# Thank You

## Carolyn Kizer

In the early sixties, when I was editing *Poetry Northwest,* I received a packet of poems from Mona Van Duyn. She said that she'd had trouble placing them because editors told her that they took up too much space. I replied that I would print them if they took up the whole magazine!—it being then, as it is today, a small volume of forty-four pages. I was totally beguiled by her poetry. Long before most poets began writing about domestic matters—"relationships" in the most inclusive meaning of that overused term; friendship, which only the T'ang poets had truly dealt with; life in suburbia, a subject which wasn't "poetic" according to the careful, elegant male poets fashionable then—Ms. Van Duyn was mistress of the world as we actually live it. Mundane!—with epigraphs from Plato, Henry James, Santayana, Norman O. Brown, Christopher Smart.

One of the poems which I published then was "Three Valentines to the Wide World." Last year, when I chose a poem of hers for inclusion in *100 Great Poems by Women,* I picked that poem, both for sentimental reasons and because I continue to adore it—which shows either my consistency of taste or Mona's enduring glory; both, I believe.

A decade later I was on the National Book Awards jury, and I had the intense pleasure of seeing her win the prize. At a celebratory dinner party, one of the guests was taking credit for having "discovered" Mona's work, at which juncture she leaned across him toward me and said pointedly that I deserved credit, which, in small part, perhaps I did. She inscribed that volume, *To See, To Take,* as follows: "For Carolyn, the earliest, most constant and the 'purest' admirer of my poems, with inexpressible gratitude and affection." (I just reread that inscription again, after many years. What joy!)

I still chortle with glee when I think of Mona's poem "Leda" (also in *If It Be Not I*). She is what I call a "hot" poet: full of passionate feeling and sensuous perception. But she is also a poet of cold nerve. Imagine not only taking on Yeats's most famous poem but doing so with complete success! The last quatrain reads:

> She tried for a while to understand what it was
>
> that had happened, and then decided to let it drop.
>
> She married a smaller man with a beaky nose,
>
> And melted away in the storm of everyday life.

And ten years on, there is the profoundly moving *Letters from a Father,* a book in which the final parent-child reconciliation is made after what must have been an unusually difficult and painful childhood. "And throughout all eternity, I forgive you, you forgive me." We're lucky if we have a lifetime in which to learn to understand. Then there was *Near Changes,* and the Pulitzer for 1991, about which Edward Hirsch said, "Mona Van Duyn has a gift for making the ordinary appear strange and for turning a common situation into a metaphysical exploration." I would amend that to say that Mona shows that the ordinary is strange, with a strangeness that only an artist can reveal to us.

Then Mona became poet laureate and in 1993 published *Firefall,* notable for its shower of minimalist sonnets, showing yet another facet of her command of form. But I still love to return to an early poem, "Open Letter, Personal" *(If It Be Not I),* that I have recited in public and to friends more times than I can count—it is Mona's great tribute to friendship, the bond which outlasts all others. Here is the last stanza:

We know the quickest way to hurt each other, and we have
used that knowledge. See, it is here, in the joined strands
of our weaknesses, that we are netted together and heave
together strongly like the great catch of mackerels that ends
an Italian movie. I feel your bodies smell and shove
and shine against me in the mess of the pitching boat.
>    My friends
we do not like each other any more. We love.

The only problem with reading that poem aloud was that it
always made me choke up. It still does.
Thank you, Mona, my friend.

# For Mona, Going On

## Richard Howard

*As for me, I lost
all sense of human possibility . . .*

*Blacking out,* we say; but it was more like
ablution in the Country of the Blue,
that region of "altogether elsewhere,"
    possibly sacred . . .
Arriving hungry after airborne hours
for a Poetry Festival, I had
fainted among my fellow bards, offstage.
    Out of the blue, then,
came (before I could recognize your face)
your voice, incredulous squeal that oddly
mixed with carpet-figures and the fragrance
    of Spray-O-Vac Rose:

"Richard, *you* passed out!" The accusation
was evident: any *evanouissement*
to be sanctioned here was really your thing,
    and my spill or spell
on the floor—though I had no notion of

its drama at the time: leave that to you!—
was probably a version of that same
    "drive for attention"
to which, mother said, I was always prone
(surely the *mot juste* now). In any case,
I knew I had no such visible contacts
    with the Other Side,

no likely means of recuperating
messages left indecipherable
unless I put myself to Mona's School:
    where else grapple with
such hard-won experience, no sooner gained
than gainsaid by means of your so-envied
rhetorical conversion-hysteria.
    Such was the lesson
of your lyceum—no wonder you laid claim
or likely connoisseurship at the least
to these episodes of "fallings from us" . . .
    In a life given

to any of these obliterations,
to debility, danger and despair,
*let it come down!* as the Second Murderer
    famously remarks;
make no attempt to spare anyone grief,
but Go For It, fail without fail, settle
down at the center of the worst and wait
    there for whatever
news we never hoped or hated to hear

half so much, despatches you especially
listened for and lovingly retrieved: not
    to know anything,

but only to be looking for something,
renouncing the possession of wisdom
in favor of the power to observe.
    Most of us, Mona,
spoil our poems (our lives) because we have
ideas—not ideas but approved topics
that can be carried around intact. Oh
    watch me faint once more,
and this time make a true recovery:
acceptance of the vast erroneous
community of pain to which we all
    belong. No ideas

but in nothing! No failures but those proved!
*To become* poets, *to become* human,
never *to be,* for as soon as we "are"
    we are no longer
human perhaps, nor even poets . . . Once
I had come to, I obeyed Van Duyn's Law:
we only are by virtue of (it *is*
    a virtue, I guess)
our continual tendency not to be . . .
You scraped me off the floor, and we performed
our poems in a state of perfect health—
    until the next time.

# II ⧜ Discussions

# Blood, Toil, Tears, Sweat, and Soup

## Stephen Yenser

Early in the course of imagining this essay, I was interested to find myself thinking repeatedly how much Wordsworth would have— or by my belated, incandescent lights should have—approved of Mona Van Duyn's project. Of her subject matter, for one thing— at least if he could have brought himself to tolerate life in the suburbs of the nefarious city—because in her work we find such inveterate concern with the "incidents and situations from common life" that he considered a desideratum. From renewing her driver's license to sunbathing on the patio, from walking her dog to riding through an automatic carwash or lying wretchedly in bed with her flu-ridden husband, no part of the ordinary world—and especially the gritty, sweaty, domestic sector—is beyond her poetic ken or blessing. A native of Eldora, Iowa, a longtime resident of St. Louis, and a teacher at Washington University, she is a deep-dyed Midwesterner, and she has a profound understanding of the inhabitants of the Missouri Ozarks and of the towns she whisks us through in "A Small Excursion" *(If It Be Not I)*—towns with mulishly immiscible names like Bourbon and Bean Lake, Chloride and Gumbo. Her "The Hermit of Hudson Pond" is a not too distant relative of the old leech-gatherer and Michael. It is characteristic of her that she would be inspired, not to an intricate meditation by a Mannerist portrait in a convex mirror, but to a terse interpretation of Goya's painting "Two Old People Eating Soup" *(If It Be Not I)*.

Wordsworth's notorious demand for "a language really used by men," not to mention women, and for a "plainer and more emphatic" poetic mode is also answered by her poems. Workaday, uneducated speech seems the very medium of some of them, including those in *Letters from a Father*, with their awkward front porch fluency invisibly reconstructed. And in *Bedtime Stories*, the stories of an immigrant grandmother, with her make-do syntax and stopgap grammar, become in this poet's hands the opportunity for a unique economy. We also hear from time to time the even "plainer and more emphatic language" of the animal and the mechanical worlds, for Van Duyn's poems are also a Cagey recollection of everyday's raucous music—the baying of a pet coonhound, the rude eructation of an exhibitionistically revved motorcycle, the bray of a lottery ticket saleswoman, the desperate bawl of a cow in heat—all of it set down on the page in sounds hitherto unspent.

When she is *not* sounding like these others, she sounds like no one else writing poems just now, even when she speaks as Cinderella or as Lot's wife, although her own language is paradoxically so unaffected that again I think of her precursor's contempt for what he called "the gaudy and inane phraseology of many modern writers." Which is to say that her poems are fiercely, doggedly, unmistakably honest, and therefore utterly personal. No one else would see things just as she does when she finds herself in rural Maine, her lake country, in her poem "West Branch Ponds, Kokadju, Maine" *(If It Be Not I)*—not far from the imagery of suburban life even here—stepping over "burned pizzas / dropped among blooms by the lone cow." Perhaps the same cow, perhaps the same Blossom for whom she has named a ballad *(If It Be Not I)*, lies in "Moose in the Morning, Northern Maine" *(If It Be Not I)* with "her bones pointing this way and that, / . . . collapsed like a badly constructed / pup tent in the dark weeds." And then there is "The pond, like a great pan of broth, [that] bubbles with feeding trout when the hatch comes on." Before long, she herself will enter, "peeling, bobbing on top, grim, / the cookpot of the trout pond, with its scalloped, / smoky rim," with the double result that "Now we are all together in the stew" *(If It Be Not I)*.

But perhaps this is to make Van Duyn seem a kind of chef, a calculating creator of products intended to seduce consumers, a domesticator of the first water. Or stock. In fact, far from being a genie of the domicile, she is as responsible as any recent poet for bringing to our attention the deliquescent, catabolic, chaotic nature of things, as her poem "A Time of Bees" *(If It Be Not I)* so vividly indicated early on. In a fashion that will come to be characteristic, this poem contrasts the masculine, scientific, probing intellect with the feminine, sensuous, responsive sensibility. The speaker and her husband, plagued by bees year after year, finally succeed in rooting out the nest hidden behind a wall of the house. Or her husband does, at any rate; his virile, "fierce / sallies . . . inspections, cracks located / and sealed, insecticides shot" have constituted their side of the battle year in and year out. Having reached at last the source,

> He calls me, and I march
>
> from a dream of bees to see them, winged and unwinged,
> such a mess of interrupted life dumped on newspapers—
> dirty clots of grubs, sawdust, stuck fliers, all smeared
> together with old honey, they writhe, some of them, but
>> who cares?
> They go to the garbage, it is over, everything has been said.

But that is not after all the end of the story. That night the speaker and her husband go to a party where they meet a research pharmacologist in search of a quantity of "an enzyme in the flight-wing muscle" of the honeybee. They take the pharmacologist back to their home, their garbage can, and the bees:

> The dead are darker, but the others have
> moved in the ooze toward the next moment. My God
> one half-worm gets its wings right before our eyes.
> Searching fingers sort and lay bare, they need
> the idea of bees—and yet, under their touch, the craze
>
> for life gets stronger in the squirming, whitish kind.
> The men do it. Making a claim on the future, as love
> makes a claim on the future, grasping. And I, underhand,
> I feel it start, a terrible, lifelong heave
> taking direction. Unpleading, the men prod
>
> till all that grubby softness wants to give, *to give.*

At such a juncture, one cannot reasonably separate intellectual curiosity from erotic experiment, basic revulsion from orgasmic acceptance, or indeed death from life. It is the representation of this "mess" of compelling forces that seems to me characteristic of Van Duyn's poems.

At the end of her first collected poems, *Merciful Disguises,* there comes a poem entitled "Walking the Dog: A Diatribe" (also in *If It Be Not I*). When I reviewed that volume years ago, I wrote little about this concluding poem, even though my review had to do in part with Van Duyn's suburban subject matter and even though here was a poem sharply aware of orderly hedges and tree rows and embarrassingly "clattery trash" exiled to the curbs. I mentioned a dainty *trouvaille* or two, including "the girlish swish" of passing automobile tires, but I turned aside from the poem as a whole—largely, I now think, because I was insufficiently attentive to the *other* side of that suburban domesticity, Van Duyn's treatment of which had so enthralled me.

Today's myopia, in contrast, leads me to believe that "Walking the Dog: A Diatribe" has to do with the unequal antagonism between the domesticating impulse and the nature of things to which that impulse responds. To write about that poem would have been to acknowledge its recognition of the superior power of the unknowable "natural," the ineffably inhuman, the fundamentally chaotic. The theme is there on the surface of things, it now seems to me, in the difference between the utterly "self-absorbed," unseen (and in effect unseeable) cicadas, with their overwhelming droning, and the coonhound, "whose throat [is] shaped for sounding the hunt." It is there in the difference between the "sidewalk," with its "plantings of pyracantha" that guard private property, and the "gross / distortion of shapes and shadows which lunge in the light-and-black / of night and storm and one streetlamp." It is there in the difference between the bourgeois rite of exercising the family pet and the blunt affront of "the violent evening," the "dark / where there are no forms." When Van Duyn's speaker tells us, "Back home, my skin crawls with the sense that I've been through something," she has in mind an encounter with the utterly Other; and though she says that, as she "brush[es] at the invisible / felt facts of [her] journey," she is "hoping to finger webs, threads, spiders, worms," she is aware instead of the abyss that such webs temporarily span. One word for this formless otherness is of course *death,* which is why her skin "crawls."

Another name for it is perhaps the *abject.* Certainly the image that our contemporary connoisseur of the condition, Julia Kristeva, in her *Powers of Horror,* conjures to represent the abject comports with Van Duyn's blind, stormy night: in Kristeva's metaphor, the abject is "A night without images but buffeted by black sounds." The abject, from Kristeva's point of view, is not just contrary to the subject and all its formalizing tendencies (evident even in such tidy concepts as "subject"), since in a sense any "object" is contrary to (if thus, however, "homologous" with) its "subject," but is the annihilation of the subject. The "abject," in other words, is what undermines if it has not already precluded "identity, system, order. What does not respect borders, positions, rules." The abject is thus associated with that which the subject would cast off. Indeed, *abject* derives from Latin roots meaning *to throw away*—rather as *diatribe,* it now occurs to me, derives from Greek roots meaning *to abrade or to wear away.* Such rejected materials might include, for instance, dung and food (which are after all, as the alchemists knew, basically one) and refuse of all kinds (orts, offal, urine, menses, pus, nail parings, perhaps even sweat, smegma, sperm, tears, saliva). The rejected materials, from the subject's blinkered point of view, are the abject; the *I,* in contrast, depends upon precisely the exclusion of such amorphous, ephemeral materials—materials that would dissolve the "self" back into its fundamental animality, its basic amniotic fluids and chemical soups.

Well, we've come a long, extravagant way from Van Duyn's secular dark night of the soul in "Walking the Dog: A Diatribe"—and yet, even as I enter that caveat, I think of the remarkable frequency of bodily fluids in her work, and I remember the virtual magnetism for her of images of the lake, the pond, and the marsh, and I call up *Letters from a Father,* with its multifarious ulcerations, bleedings, bowel movements, indigestions, scabs, warts, and so on. In fact, if I let myself dwell on the subject, I can imagine Van Duyn as a kind of spiritual sister of Doctor Matthew O'Connor in Djuna Barnes's *Nightwood.* The doctor is forever associated, in the minds of many who have been ensnared by that novel, with his "appallingly degraded" Paris *grenier,* overflowing with his abortionist's tools, books, perfumes, and on and on, all epitomized by "A swill-pail [that] stood at the head of [his] bed, brimming with abominations." If the comparison with Barnes tends to overstatement, perhaps that is because I suspect a younger self of having erred in the other direction, as though Van Duyn were all about delicate perceptions ("girlish swish" indeed!) and observations regarding neighborhood barbecues. It is indeed these things—she's not kidding when somewhere in *Near Changes* she eulogizes "the sweet quotidian"—but it's clear enough today that she means her poetry to include as much as possible of life as she knows it. Because she rhymes a lot, composes sestinas and villanelles, and tirelessly invents her own prosodic forms, and because there is a tendency abroad—among those who think in such terms—to associate the serious use of such forms with "doily-making," we might be too quick to think of her as fastidious, exclusionary, precious, exacting. In fact, she is more Whitmanian than Dickinsonian, more Poundian that Oppenian, more like Myna Low than Lorrine Niedecker. I have no idea what she thinks of Louise Gluck's work, but I wouldn't be surprised if she found it undernourished or costive; at the same time, however, while I have no idea what she thinks of Sharon Olds's poems either, I'd guess that she might find them gushy and formless.

I suddenly find myself on the brink of arguing that she is a kind of middle-of-the-road writer, a Midwestern mean between the boarding school and the bearshit-on-the-trail school. While it's true that I can almost think of her as no less "cooked" than "raw," to cadge Levi-Straus's famous terms once more, she seems to me primarily the latter. Kristeva would associate her with the feminine, "nurturing horror" beneath civilization's symbolic, "cunning, orderly surface." For Kristeva that association would involve the maternal, and Van Duyn is expressly childless (she dedicated *Near Changes* to her husband, Jarvis Thurston, and her friends, "who fill to the brim a life empty of family"; and a number of poems, ranging from the poignantly frank "Words for the Dumb" to the allegorical "Have You Seen Me?" both in *Firefall,* refer to what used to be called nulliparity), but the biographical circumstance is of secondary importance here.

What counts is Van Duyn's low esteem for purity, system, and conventional borders and her corresponding preference for the mixogamous, the improvised, and the transgressive. In an early poem pointedly entitled "Pot-au-Feu" *(A Time of Bees,* also in *If It Be Not I)* she implies her own affinity for the entropic Nature

GARNETT LIBRARY
SMSU-WEST PLAINS

that "feeds on trouble"and "devastation" and "love's dishevelment" and that uses "the disorder that is death to us" to produce yet "more anchovies and asparagus" (words beginning with *a* because omega yields alpha). This affinity, she claims, is feminine, since "my sex is less prone to the torment / of organic dignity, and more attached to our ferment." Like Earth herself, she vows to her husband, "I'll debase my system" and sacrifice "a feast of patterning, a treat of tended lines," to keep him fat and happy, "an inexhaustible fountain of passionate waste," while she herself will "grow and blossom on its deathly taste." At this and many other points Van Duyn casts her lot with those poets who in my view of the world adopt as their motto Holderlin's lines in his marvelous fragment on the harvest, *und ein Gesetz ist / dass alles hineingeht:* "and it's a law that everything goes in," into the universal autumnal stew. Nothing is wasted; all is plowed under.

As Van Duyn's friend James Merrill put it in "Lost in Translation," "But nothing's lost. Or else: all is translation / And every bit of us is lost in it / (Or found . . .)." Ten years or so after Merrill's poem appeared in print, Van Duyn published "Misers" (*Near Changes*—not to be confused with "The Miser" in *To See, To Take*), dedicated to Merrill. It is in seven distichs—a version of the sonnet that Merrill was partial to (cf. "The Friend of the Fourth Decade" and two sections of "The Will")—and I will quote it entire:

> On the streets of New York I've seen them rummaging,
>     the grizzled,
> the torn, grimed and scabbed by the world, their mouths
>     muzzled,
>
> misers of crust and Coke bottle, whatever is valued or needed.
> My unhelpful heart glints out at them, but is unheeded.
>
> One man we free ones cherish is freer to reassess worth.
> Miser of love and language, walking the streets of the earth,

he ransacks, ransoms what we all hold dear, then some days,
like someone who, out for a stroll, all Blackglama and Cartier,

with a collector's vision spots, in a streak of debris
on the sidewalk, a little length the poor can't use, dusty,

stranger still something unbarterable, absurd,
unneeded, unsought—like my heart or an archaic word—

he bends down and takes it, thinking, "I saw it, it is mine."
Only the rich—the gifted—know how to treasure Twine.

Merrill (whose inherited wealth made him "freer to reassess worth"
than most of us to the extent that it liberated him to appraise the
"unbarterable") surely approved the economical aptness of all this.
The couplets bring together the first and second person, the poet
and the addressee, and the frequently alliterative lines reinforce that
coupling with their own twinning and twining. In the end, she and
he intertwine: he saw her heart, she saw his, and they are two in
one. Because *twine* in a rare or "archaic" sense means *embrace*, it is
almost superfluous to note that it comes from a root that leads also
to *two* and *twain* and that is present in vestigial form in *twilight,*
*between,* and *betwixt,* as well as in *deuce, dual,* and *double.* But we
cannot overlook the last stanza's phantom rhyme, generated by the
dedication and the concluding couplet: "thine." *Mine* and *thine* and
*twine*—I notice in passing that Van Duyn begs to be factored in.

In Van Duyn's most recent book, *Firefall*—the very title of
which speaks to a marriage of seemingly antagonistic elements—
"Mr. and Mrs. Jack Sprat in the Kitchen" praises the combination
of her "searchings, revisions, / tossed with his ration / of compulsive precision," a "joint creation" that "so mimics life" it seems
"mandated / that God had a wife / who collaborated." In the same
book, "Je meurs de soif aupres de la fontaine," a masterful villanelle
written virtually in contravention of Keats's famous epitaph,
adumbrates a "green oasis where word and water marry." "Another

Tempest," if I read it aright, treats Caliban and Miranda as one figure (the offspring of Prospero), with a "love-lotioned . . . soft, slow, heavy earthliness," the twin of Ariel ("the other self") and the partner of Ferdinand. One of *Firefall*'s densest poems, "Rascasse," extols the bouillabaisse whose sine qua non is "the hog-fish, known to folk / and fishermen as the ugliest fish in the world." Both flesh and fish, so to speak, a kind of natural hippogryph, the hog-fish represents the very "essence" of being for Van Duyn. The meaning of the hog-fish is forecast by the unusual bouquet that adorns her table in the harborside restaurant in Nice. When the poet asks the *maître d'hôtel* what the flower is, he responds with what she momentarily imagines is the first-person singular pronoun in English, but then she realizes that of course he has said "ail"—and that "we have not come for charm and blossom, but homeliness, / the deep, loamy musk of birth and decay / that hides from the eyes, the head of the garlic, the seed." If our "eyes have led us astray through dreaming years, / cherishing consonance, curve, the colorful, / proportion, radiance, balance, harmony, / shapeliness that ages etched into our lenses," the hog-fish nonetheless exists to remind us of the "formless fury [that] fills earth's bowels and fuels us." The hog-fish is in effect Tennyson's "'fire in the belly'" and Yeats's "foul rag-and-bone shop of the heart." In short,

> What fertilizes but muck? What began us but slime?
> We nod to the *belle-laide* with her troublesome half-truth,
> but what gives comfort, what creates, but ugliness?

This is Van Duyn's home key, and the poem ends with a quatrain, eerily lit with grotesquerie, that could well stand at the head of her complete poems:

> The rich broth of life, whose bubble eyes
> hold both the unseen and the seen, will defend it—
> essence—ugliness (eh, *rascasse?*), comfort.
> May all the color and beauty of the world attend it!

Although in recent years Van Duyn has occasionally composed what she aptly calls "minimalist sonnets," and although she has at least pretended to weary of plenitude ("Mockingbird Month" in *Near Changes* inveighs against "the bird the Indians called 'four hundred / tongues'" because there seems to be no end to his songs and variations), she is more a maximalist than ever. Indeed, her minimalist sonnets sometimes sprout tails and become in her words "extended minimalist sonnets," and a number of her poems since those collected in *If It Be Not I* address the subject more or less explicitly. In "Lines Written in a Guest Book" *(Near Changes),* to take an instance, she contrasts the "Japanese garden" sort of poem with "another kind." In the former, a "dry hint of a river or brook" (and how dry a hint that "dry" is), "raked free of detritus, briefly flows, turns / into terraces (abstraction of waterfall) and comes to its end in a large, strict rectangle / of the same white sand (the sea, the All / or Nothingness . . .)." But she has heard the subversive *tangle* in "rectangle," if you will, and in the other kind of garden, "another poetry," we find a "'mimicry / of endlessness' [that] calls upon every muscle / of self, while the senses are whelmed toward idolatry." Remarkably reminiscent of the gardens at Appleton House as Marvell describes them (see especially the penultimate stanza of that long poem), Van Duyn's "rich acreage" includes "steeps and valleys," "a Grotto," "wild blooms under tree-shade," "a Maze," a "beautiful Folly" that might be her private synecdoche, and so on—in short, a landscape created by "loving lavishness . . . / worlds of thought and feeling as real as the world."

This is her kind of poetry—as it was the kind of poetry, at least in principle, of Howard Nemerov, her friend and colleague at Washington University. "The greatest poetry," he opined (perhaps echoing that earlier St. Louis poet T. S. Eliot—who by then in England was echoing Dame Juliana of Norwich—as well as John Stuart Mill), "sees clearly and says plainly the wickedness and terror and beauty of the world, while at the same time humming to itself, so that we overhear rather than hear: All will be well." In

Van Duyn's more circumspect words, prompted by "A Bouquet of Zinnias" *(Near Changes),*

> Utter clarity of color, as if amidst all that
> mystery inside and outside one's own skin
> this at least was something unmistakeable,
> multiplicity of both color and form, as if
> in certain parts of our personal economy
> abundance were precious—these are their two main virtues.

But clarity and abundance of color and form, *pace* this poem's preceding reservations, do not exclude appreciation of "delicacy." On the contrary, although it has been "a month of zinnias," love itself has "multitudinous uses," and just as there is another kind of garden, so there are other flowers and

> other months in the year, other levels
> of inwardness, other ways of loving. In the shade
> of my garden, leaf-sheltering lilies of the valley,
> for instance, will keep in tiny, exquisite bells
> their secret clapper. And up from my bulbs will come
> welcome Dutch irises whose transcendent blue,
> bruisable petals curve sweetly over their center.

One doesn't have to realize that Van Duyn's heritage is Dutch to see the connection. These lines testify marvelously to her love of nuance, even as they conjure without naming them aspects of female sexuality. The point, then, is to exclude *nothing,* however phallicly flagrant or clandestinely clitoral, that partakes of the world's fecundity. She pleads in *Near Changes* in "Glad Heart at the Supermarket" (a title that ironically revises that of Randall Jarrell's famous essay), when thinking about her multifarious "friends,"

> let me taste, while I'm here, the new flavors
> of otherness in your changing cases and shelves,

plucking with free, unguarded gluttony

that keeps my tongue in spiced surprise at your selves.

For we die of sameness . . .

So it is the "Abundance! Incalculable abundance" that she prizes in the world of her friends, in the supermarket of their friendship, where "at unexpected times / new ices, canned goods or sea-foods are put on show," with the result that she says, "No treat / in mind today, I picked out produce I needed," and as chance would have it, "Something called jicama rolled and fell at my feet."

To be sensitive to all of the world's activities would be intolerable, as George Eliot reminds us in *Middlemarch:* "If we had a keen vision of all ordinary life, it would be like hearing the grass grow and the squirrel's heart beat, and we should die of that roar which lies on the other side of silence. As it is, the quickest of us walk about wadded with stupidity." Similarly, if we could take in the abundance of the world, the understanding would be insupportable. We would be like the speaker in "Last Words of Pig No. 6707" *(Near Changes),* a subject in a Department of Agriculture experiment aimed at creating a superanimal with human genes; he is so fat with his awareness of the things of this world that he cannot stand or mate. He is virtually one with "the green globe" itself, or in an even more condensed term the very "glebe" of Earth, which cannot sanction the loss of "any image . . . in its purposeless play." The weight of the "packed world" is unbearable except (perhaps) by the world itself. For the most part, however, this thought is cause for celebration in Van Duyn's poems. In "Birthstones," the prefatory poem in *Near Changes,* her mother's gift of a ring that features what turns out to be an imitation emerald nevertheless (or perhaps *therefore*) teaches the poet-to-be that "the real jewel" is the planet, the only truly precious stone. Indeed this whole poem is a kind of elaboration on the buried rhyme that we hear in its last two lines: "Dazzled I walk the world my mother gave me, / whose stony streets are paved with emerald." "My green, my fluent mundo"—

Wallace Stevens addresses the same entity in "Notes toward a Supreme Fiction," where before Van Duyn he adapts Marvell's "The Garden," with its mind's happy, creative annihilation of "all that's made / To a green Thought in a green Shade."

Van Duyn's intermittent paean to Earth takes the form in "The Ferris Wheel" *(Near Changes)* of a sensibility divided between the ride's passenger's "transcendences," during which her look downward at the lights permits a paradoxical vision of a seeming "heaven on earth" (at this height absent are the carnival's actual fistfights and "ladies of the night," and absent, too, the male operator and by extension all the masculine "fingers firmed by placards, voting levers, / hammer and tongs, steeringwheels, gavels," and "eyes still fit for bombsights"). Her belief is that "common human kindness" alone (with its acknowledgement of the importance of life in the stews, if you will) allows "the only life worth living, the empathic life." In the end, with her grocery bag full of "root vegetables" and other ingredients for an "age-old stew," she is Mona Van Duyn, the passenger who "counts on gravity to bring her back / finally, and for good, to the fairground." Back to the pied carnival the world is, that is to say, and back also to the bedrock that is (to suspend emotional gravity for the nonce) the fairground of Earth. "The world's perverse," as she puts it in "Sonnet for Minimalists" *(Near Changes)*—a mini-hymn to the ever-burgeoning Earth, in which she implicitly reveals both the etymological link between *paean,* Apollo's epithet in the "Hymn for Apollo," and *peony,* and the virtual synonymity in turn of *peony* and *anthem*—"but it could be worse." It could also be verse, since in their different ways both earth and verse entail a turning (*verse* is of course from *vertere,* "to turn," especially a plow, in arable ground), or indeed a troping (from *tropos,* as is *heliotrope,* the flower that turns toward Apollo).

One version of that last flower is the subject of Van Duyn's brilliant villanelle, "On a Majolica Sunflower Plate: American, Early 1880's" *(Near Changes),* which is another hymn to the sun god, as well as an ode to the Kansas state flower. A poem that should be read in light of Merrill's "Syrinx" and Keats's "Ode on a Grecian Urn" and no doubt several other ekphrastic lyrics (as well as Blake's "Ah, Sunflower" and Stevens's "Sunday Morning"), "On a Majolica Sunflower Plate" compresses the myth of Apollo and Leucothea, who was abandoned by the god and was turned into the sunflower, with the making—i.e., the glazing, the rich decorating, and the *firing*—of a piece of majolica that is for many intents and purposes contiguous with its representation of a sunflower. In Van Duyn's poem the sunflower's "face" (or the plate) offers "the food of song" because its seeds, blistered by the sky from "green to black," nourish the birds (mockingbirds, since we're in Kansas) and thus seed "the sky with notes the earth mislaid." The villanelle form—itself suggestive by way of its intricacy of majolica patterns—is superbly suited to the subject, partly because its refrains or transumptions reinforce both the flower's "seeding [of] the sky with notes" and the birds' reseeding of the ground with sunflowers. Because the seeds need the sun to grow into flowers, Leucothea and Apollo achieve a marriage after all. Not that Van Duyn ever lets us overlook the irony of the rhyme of "hymn" with "him," since there is a sense in which the *hymn*, the song, is the antonym of the *him, the god, who rejected her.*

But *"it's a law that everything goes in, / pythonic, prophetic . . ."* Holderlin's rule for the cosmic mulligatawny is Van Duyn's for the *pot-au-feu* of marriage—the departure point for so many of her poems—marriage, which is at bottom her trope for the self's ideal relationship to the world, with which she would replace the Christian figure of the self's relationship to the savior or the other world. Van Duyn is incorrigibly worldly, perhaps not sophisticated (she knowingly refers to herself in "Homework" *[To See, To Take]* as a "sweating Proust of the pantry shelves" and insists that we hear the domestic's pant in "pantry"), but worldly—and pragmatical, therefore, and resourceful. In "The Marriage Sculptor" *(Firefall),* a recent poem among so many of hers that deal with connubial adjustments, "the old master" who made a "late work" on the subject of marriage ("so fine the embrace of spirits, so expressive the bright pour / of leaning lights, so rich the exchanging changes") is confronted with its utter destruction as the result of this or that lightning bolt. In the true Yeatsian spirit—"All things fall, and are built again, / And those who build them again are gay"—the sculptor turns his attention to his "materials, safe," even though his group sculpture has been destroyed. His single question is, What to make of those materials now? How—since "nothing human is perfect"—to "shelter the next [form] from storm?" I cannot do better than quote the last six lines of this poem:

> He spoke tenderly to his elements: "Beauty
> learns from beauty, the first costly form
>
> lies coiled in the last." Then, "I am not Eros.
> Since Time is made out of it (who calls himself
> king) the human stuff I work with is stronger than
> Time," he said to us, who thought we had lost something.

But—we realize anew—nothing's lost, and that is thanks to Mona Van Duyn, her generation's mother of us all, and her tradition.

# The Bowl Glows Gold: An Appreciation of Mona Van Duyn

Rachel Hadas

Let's start in the kitchen.

### Mr. and Mrs. Jack Sprat in the Kitchen

"About half a box,"
I say, and the male
weighs his pasta sticks
on our postal scale.

To support my sauce
of a guesswork rhymer
he boils by the laws
of electric timer.

Our joint creation,
my searchings, revisions
tossed with his ration
of compulsive precisions,

so mimics life
we believe it mandated

that God had a wife
who collaborated.

And cracked, scraped, old,
still the bowl glows gold.

*(Firefall)*

At issue are the shared but contrasting joint preparation of a meal, the different ways men and women go about doing things, affection, time, Adam and Eve—a hundred pages' worth of experience and wry wisdom boiled down into laconic quatrains and topped off with a title that glances at a nursery rhyme. Very big and very small, domestic and cosmic—welcome to the world of Mona Van Duyn.

This world may seem cozy, but you need to keep your eyes open. The rich images in which Van Duyn's work abounds may be (to use the title phrase of her 1973 collection) merciful disguises. Flowers, birds, landscapes, food—how pleasurable, how immediately recognizable! But they're sneaky. If you read these poems with what Blake called single vision, then you are in danger of failing what Van Duyn, in a poem of that title, calls the Vision Test. Yes, the test in question is a real test that the poet must take when her "license is lapsing." But it is also more, or other, than that. For example, are we speaking of a driver's license here? And who is being tested? The applicant who must "master a lighted box of far or near" or the lady who administers the test, the "kindly priestess" with "her large, / round face, her vanilla pudding, baked-apple-and-spice / face in continual smiles"—a figure who before the end of the poem has been transformed into a "hen drinking clotted milk"? This test-giver (she has found the profession "poet" to be hilarious) is loth, as the actual test begins at the close of the poem, to administer it, for there is no telling how a poet will interpret the world:

Her pencil trembles,
then with an almost comically obvious show

of reluctance she lets me look in her box of symbols
for normal people who know where they want to go.

Earlier in "The Vision Test" *(If It Be Not I)*, the speaker has imagined the others being tested as children who "come to grips with the rocks / and scissors of the world" at the maternal hands of the test-giver. But I am also rather tempted to envision these "normal people who know where they want to go" as male. In Van Duyn's 1993 Library of Congress lecture, "Matters of Poetry," she tells us that certain male critics have been deceived by the domestic disguises in which her imagery is so rich into believing that her poems are only about the sources of their metaphors. As indeed they are—birds and bees, flowers and food, pantries and cabins. But they are also always about more.

> Ever since high school I have enjoyed writing extended metaphor poems, writing about one thing in terms of another, which gives me a chance to play with the double meanings of words which can work simultaneously on both sides of the metaphor . . . Blinded by the assumption that women do not have thoughts, do not write about ideas, reviewers who are incredibly talented at understanding the most difficult and private poetry by members of their own sex announce blithely that a poem of mine about the need for form in life and art is about walking a dog, or an analysis of friendship is about shopping for groceries.

Critics who cannot see Van Duyn's doublenesses surely fail her Vision Test.

Van Duyn's wise, funny, piquant poems are distinctive, but they are not freakish or unique. Should we place her in a tradition of female domestic poetry? In "Matters of Poetry" she writes rather impatiently, "Of course I write poems about everyday life—home, family, loved ones—every poet does, male or female." The nature of the imagery and her distrust of abstractions are sometimes posited as explicitly female (as in "Mr. and Mrs. Jack Sprat"), but not always:

> I have never enjoyed those roadside overlooks from which
> you can see the mountains of two states. The view keeps
>    generating
> a kind of pure, meaningless exaltation
> that I can't find a use for. It drifts away from things . . .
>    into a statement so abstract
> that it's tiresome. Nothing particular holds still in it.

("Three Valentines to the Wide World," *If It Be Not I*)

In her preference for what reaches us through our senses over abstract formulations that "drift away from things," Van Duyn can of course be placed in a tradition of women's poetry that would surely include Elizabeth Bishop and May Swenson. But she has other less obvious affinities too. Reading through Van Duyn's *oeuvre* recently, I kept being reminded of another writer. Who was it? I soon realized that Van Duyn's robust and witty sensuousness and her agile use of imagery "which can work simultaneously on both sides of the metaphor" recall Aristophanes, the sublime comic poet of fifth-century Athens. Like Van Duyn, Aristophanes, allergic to resounding abstractions and possessed of an allegorical bent, would pass the Vision Test with flying colors. Like Van Duyn, he can seem to be poking around the larder when his real subject is how to write a play or how to stop a war. For, again like Van Duyn, Aristophanes isn't shy about tackling such undomestic topics as poetry or peace.

Looking through Aristophanes in search of a few specific instances of this unexpected but enchanting poetic kinship, I had the pleasant experience of refreshing my acquaintance with one of the funniest and slipperiest of great writers—a delight for which I am indebted to Mona Van Duyn. Three examples, culled from only two plays, will have to suffice to illustrate my sense of the parallels between these two poets (I hesitate to use the word "tradition," though the tradition, if there is one, is comic—one could explore Shakespeare, Moliere, and so on). The translation by the ingenious nineteenth-century British cleric Benjamin Bickley Rogers has a jolly Gilbert and Sullivan flavor; Aristophanes' Greek uses far fewer words, giving the sense of a sketchier style and a more colloquial, fluent pace. But Rogers to my ear best conveys Aristophanes' wit.

In Aristophanes' *The Frogs,* Euripides, competing with Aeschylus in a contest as to who is the superior tragedian, claims that he has dieted down the tragic art from the bloated condition in which Aeschylus left it:

> When first I took the art from you, bloated and swoln, poor
> thing,
> With turgid gasconading words and heavy dieting,
> First I reduced and toned her down, and made her slim and neat
> With wordlets and with exercise and poultices of beet,
> And next a dose of chatterjuice distilled from books I gave her . . .

> *(939–43)*

Of course the comparison of tragedy—its theory and practice—to a patient in need of a healthful regimen is a cartoonlike allegory. But the cameo is so vivid that for a moment we forget about aesthetics and concentrate on the poor bloated girl of this before-and-after picture. Homeric similes work that way too, and so, often, do Van Duyn's poems; the scene or situation which is brought into being merely to vivify a comparison swiftly takes on an intense if miniature life of its own. The evoked scene can be tiny, as in these lines from "In the Hospital for Tests" *(If It Be Not I)*:

> In twenty-four hours, the hefty nurse, all smiles,
> carries out my urine on her hip like a jug of cider,
> a happy harvest scene.

Or it can develop into a complex vision, as, in "Passing Thought" *(Firefall)*, the image of the sea, itself a metaphor for all that is mysterious, profound, and changeable and to which the poet must (in her vision test!) be attentive, subtly shifts and grows:

> It must be peaceful to come to the end
> of the writing, or need for writing, poems,
> to wholly let go, like a cat on a lap,
> heavy and boneless as unbaked bread dough,
> of that constant attentiveness to the sea,
> all weathers and tides, its bland seething.
> Alert as if no others watched,
> as if there had never been another
> watcher, driven to know precisely
> what is being uncovered or covered
> if its near, sluggish graceless barings
> show glint, slither, in the old weeds,
> or afar, if from under the dark spread
> with its tiny wavery quilting, there erupts
> something that ducks down under again.

The sea doesn't stop there; the next few lines feature "mollusc, red-worm, mermaid, monster." But all these signify something else—as do the solidly domestic cat and dough with which the poem begins. From larder and pantry to the stretches of the unconscious—this bravura leap, composed of familiar details yet taking us out of the realm of the familiar, is what Aristophanes does, too.

A little later in *The Frogs,* for example, when Euripides boasts that his tragedies have taught the Athenians to be more canny in their household arrangements, Dionysus enthusiastically agrees with him in a passage that a single-visioned reader might easily mistake for a mere domestic riff. Note how Euripides' use of the single word "households" gives rise to a thumbnail sketch of groceries, china cupboard, and so on, which is both itself and something more:

> Eur.  I taught them all these knowing ways
>         By chopping logic in my plays,

And making all my speakers try
To reason out the How and Why.
So now the people trace the springs,
The sources and the roots of things,
And manage all their households too
Far better than they used to do,
Scanning and searching What's amiss?
And, Why was that? And, How is this?

Dio. Ay, truly, never now a man
Comes home, but he begins to scan;
And to his household loudly cries,
Why, where's my pitcher? What's the matter?
'Tis dead and gone my last year's platter.
Who gnawed these olives? Bless the spray,
Who nibbled off the head of that?
And where's the garlic vanished, pray,
I purchased only yesterday?

*(975–88)*

Those olives and garlic, that nibbled fish would be right at home in a Van Duyn poem. They are so vividly themselves that I feel I've spied a fifth-century shopping list, and yet the point being made goes beyond crockery and sprats.

The punlike wit of doubleness is one of the many pleasures of reading Van Duyn; as she has told us in the lecture, it has also been one of her pleasures as a writer since the beginning of her career. A relatively lighthearted example, too long to quote in full, is "Emergency Room," subtitled "Turnpike, Anywhere, U.S.A." *(Firefall)*.

Left on a table to die, a sandwich
can hardly believe this has happened to him.
Having heard it said so often about

his friends and neighbors, he still never expected
his own epitaph to be:
"They opened him up, took one look,
and just closed him up again."

In an adjoining section sufferers can see
disjointed bits of medical training taking place.
A long, nearly unmoving queue of them
suggests that primarily women, these days,
wish to be surgeons.
Each comes out, after what must have been
a long, laborious scrub,
looking annoyed, holding her dripping hands
well away from body and shoulderbag,
shaking them violently to dry in the air,
since the snappers-on of the rubber gloves
must be practicing someplace else.

Double vision again: the sandwich casts light on the patient, the
women on the surgeon, and vice versa. Vivid, rueful, minutely
observed—it is funny, but also not merely funny.

A third and final example from Aristophanes that savors of
Van Duyn is the passage in Lysistrata where the heroine uses the
example of spinning and weaving (quintessentially women's work)
to get a sense of political process, as it might ideally be practiced by
the war-weary women of Greece, through a male official's thick head:

> Ly.  Just as a woman, with nimble dexterity, thus with her
>              hands disentangles a skein,
>        Hither and thither her spindles unravel it, drawing it out,
>              and pulling it plain.
>        So would this weary Hellenic entanglement soon be
>              resolved by our womanly care,

So would our embassies neatly unravel it, drawing it here
    and pulling it there.

Mag. Wonderful, marvelous feats, not a doubt of it, you with
        your skeins and your spindles can show;
    Fools! do you really expect to unravel a terrible war like a
        bundle of tow?

*(567–72)*

The magistrate has no patience either for Lysistrata's trope or for
the laborious process she outlines for him—both sound too much
like work, whether mental or manual. In the words of a Van Duyn
poem I have already cited, "Its view is simultaneous / discovery
and reminiscence. It starts with the creature / and stays there,
assuming creation is worth the time / it takes . . ." "It" here is the
poem, whose double gesture (reaching into the past for knowledge
that can be applied to the future; reaching into memory for something to compare with something else) is exactly what Lysistrata
is executing in a way so offensive to the magistrate.

I have not even touched on many aspects of Van Duyn's work,
such as the range of her imagery; what Cynthia Zarin has called
her "thematic ambition"; her skill (unique, I think, among her con-
temporaries) as a writer of elegiac, celebratory, or other occasional
poetry; her learning; her humor; her heartbroken zest for the
things of this world; her recreation and preservation of her grandmother's bedtime stories. I've wanted to limit myself to such small
matters as food, laughter, and tears; and even here my thoughts
encompass much less than these subjects demand.

Food, then—two of the three examples cited from Aristophanes
touch upon nutrition-poor, overweight tragedy (until Euripides got
to her) and the Athenian householder's olives, fish, and garlic. If

food, in its earthiness, is an essential ingredient of the comic vision, it isn't, in Van Duyn's work, ever only comic or comforting or familiar. (Van Duyn's beloved friend James Merrill knew that the answer is always YES and NO.) We've already seen that the wholesome face ("baked-apple-and-spice, vanilla pudding") in "The Vision Test" masks something at best bleak, at worst actively hostile. And blandly appetizing nursery food plays an unforgettable if unobtrusive role in two poems which deal with the world of such food—the relation of daughter to mother, childhood to old age, memory. In "The Stream" *(If It Be Not I)*, the daughter takes her mother out to lunch, though "out" is inside the nursing home. The narrative fluency and ease of the following passage (reluctantly lifted from a poem too long to quote in full), its accommodation of details like cake and milk, move the reader toward the inevitable end as unconsciously, almost reassuringly, as every daily bite takes every one of us closer to our last supper.

> But they came with the lunch and card table and chairs
> and bustled and soothed you and you forgot the fears
>
> and began to eat. The white tablecloth, the separate
> plate for salad, the silvery little coffee pot,
>
> the covers for dishes must have made you feel
> you were in a restaurant again after all
>
> those shut-in years. (Dad would never spend the money,
> but long ago you loved to eat out with me.)
>
> You cleaned your soup bowl and dishes, one by one,
> and kept saying, "This is fun! This is *fun!*"
>
> The cake fell from your trembly fork, so I fed
> it to you. "Do you want mine too?" "Yes," you said,
>
> "and I'll drink your milk if you don't want it." (You'd
> lost twelve pounds already by refusing your food.)

I wheeled you back. "Well, I never did *that* before!
Thank you, Jane." "We'll do it again." "Way down *there*,"

you marveled. You thanked me twice more. My eyes were wet.
"You're welcome, Mother. You'll have a good nap now, I bet."

I arranged for your old companion, who came twice a day,
to bring you milkshakes, and reached the end of my stay.

Twenty-two lines later, word comes that the mother has died, and the poem shifts, as it were, underground, to a meditation about the subterranean nature of love—a meditation which would not be anything like as moving without the lunch that precedes it. To read Van Duyn is less to marvel at how much she gets into her poems, so natural do they seem, than to be reminded of how very much of life most poets leave out.

"Delivery," the eloquent concluding poem of *Firefall* (1993), which takes place at the other end of life from "The Stream," features some of the same characters and even some of the same food. But the nourishing meal this time is a prelude not to death but to a kind of birth. If "The Stream" is sad, "Delivery" is uncanny. With utter lack of sentimentality, it notes the cruelty of adults, the confusion of childhood, the violence of revelation. Again, the poem is too long to quote in full. In the first stanza the speaker remembers being five years old and weeping when not she herself but her friend Betty is scolded. This mix-up her mother finds funny and duly reports to the father in the second stanza:

Soon it is supper time. In the kitchen they feed
and talk, while I, invisible as I was
in high-chair days, silently sit on Sears,
wearing the weight of my big and bigger ears.
"Well, you'll never guess what your crazy kid did today—
if that wasn't the limit!" The story swells
into ache in my stomach, then Dad's laughter and hers

> slice and tear like knives and forks and a worse
> hurt is opening in my middle; in familiar
> smells and muddle of voices, mashed potatoes,
> dimming light, hamburger, thick creamed corn,
> the milk-white chill, a self is being born.
>
> And is swept away through seething clots of minnow
> in the nearly hidden creek that weeps through the meadow . . .

And we are back in the subaqueous mysteries of subliminal feeling and uncontrollable change, the flow of emotions underlying the creamed corn and cold milk. Again, two worlds are here; this remarkable poem would be the poorer were either to be left out.

Finally, from the rich and varied bill of fare that could be gleaned from Van Duyn's poems, I choose not the ugly and seductive "Rascasse" *(Firefall),* the appetizing "Salewomen in Baker Shops," or the stunningly observed and imagined "Goya's 'Two Old People Eating Soup'" (both in *If It Be Not I* ), but a passing reference to chowder. The narrative mastery of "The Stream" is in evidence here, too; the chowder isn't pressed into service as a trope, though of course it is a trope, but rather serves to introduce a heroic story of the birth of the child who gives the poem its title, "For Julia Li Qiu" *(Firefall).*

> Ten days before we expected you, we gave
> your mother and father fish and shrimp chowder
> (in carp bowls, with Cloud Ears swimming in it darkly
> —a bow to your heritage) lemon pie and tea.
>
> Next morning, early, the telephone: "Surprise!
> We're in the labor room. Water broke.
> I think baby want chowder, want to come quickly,
> but may take twenty-four hours. Talk now to Lili."

The birth turns out to be a terribly difficult one; "nothing the childbirth classes taught them came true." While the mother labors, the baby's poet father coaxes the infant along by naming all the world's beauties, in gorgeous lines that, according to the speaker, "friendship's telephone let me hear." But these lines are clearly Van Duyn's lovingly embellished version—her valentine, on Julia's behalf, to the world—of a summons whose crux we have already encountered: "I think baby want chowder, want to come quickly." For the chowder and pie and tea stand for the varied nourishment this world offers. No wonder reading Van Duyn never fails to make me hungry.

Here are two quatrains of the incantation the speaker puts into the father's mouth, translating his loving words in whatever tongue into the lingua franca of feeling but also into the idiom of English verse:

> "Come to the garden of life, its stony walkways
> through rampant blossoms of glory and peace, its dappled
> light and shade for the spirit's exquisite wooing.
> There is nothing for you in death's dark fields of undoing.

> "Come, come to love's tragi-comedy,
> the masterpiece re-written for every body
> and soul, its tears and laughter as near to each other
> as Hell and Heaven are, as lover and brother.

At Sewanee a few years ago, when Wyatt Prunty did a superb job of reading "The Vision Test" out loud, everyone in the audience howled with laughter. Van Duyn often makes me chuckle inwardly, too—a much harder feat to accomplish. And last week, sitting in the sun rereading *The Frogs* and *Lysistrata* and confirming the affinities between Aristophanes's unforgettable imagery and Van Duyn's double vision, her "metaphors that make us meld" ("For Julia Li Qiu" again), I smiled with the joy of "simultaneous / discovery and reminiscence," as Van Duyn puts it in "Three Valentines to the Wide World."

"The Stream," on the other hand, and "For Julia Li Qiu" never fail—not on first reading, nor second, nor on umpteenth reading just this minute—to fill my eyes with tears. Haven't I just been instructed that "tears and laughter [are] as near to each other / as Hell and Heaven are, as lover and brother"? I am instructed and moved, admiring this easy-seeming mastery. Above all I am grateful for the sense of renewal with which Van Duyn's marvelous poems endow me. Let me return in closing to the just-quoted valentine, twisting the line a little to say with perfect sincerity that I've never seen anything like Van Duyn's poems "for making [me] think that to spend [my] life on such old premises is a privilege."

# Mrs. Thurston's Neighborhood: A Sense of Place in the Poetry of Mona Van Duyn

Emily Grosholz

## I.

Along with her husband, Jarvis Thurston, Mona Van Duyn lives, and has lived for a long time, in a modest middle-class neighborhood near Washington University in St. Louis. The houses are solidly built, Midwestern in style, with lots in back that are half a block deep. From this plot of house and garden, sidewalk and lawn, Van Duyn has fashioned her own distinctive poetic perspective. So centered, she intends not so much to convey "local color," but to examine the realities of a life that is thoroughly planted in space and time. The constancy of her circumstances allows her to register precisely fine variations in the development of her marriage and her intimate or sociable friendships. Her exploration of a heartland that includes but goes much deeper than St. Louis and its surrounding riverine landscape is like the recurrent labor of a gardener. She belongs to the place she writes about and changes its profile slowly, with art.

 To the American homeowner who usually doesn't erect a high stone wall, the garden and yard are ambiguous parts of the property.

Inside the house, life is private, enclosed by walls and veiled by curtains at the windows. Outside, one is still on one's own ground, but exposed to the view of neighbors and stray transients, whoever happens to be passing by. Mona Van Duyn has observed that her poems have a double topic: many of the poems about her garden are at the same time meditations on marriage which half reveal, half conceal their intent.

"Notes from a Suburban Heart" *(A Time of Bees,* 1964, also in *If It Be Not I)* begins with a bit of local color anticipated and remembered as winter turns into spring.

> It's time to put fertilizer on the grass again.
> The last time I bought it, the stuff was smelly and black,
> and said "made from Philadelphia sewage" on the sack.
> It's true that the grass shot up in a violent green,
> but my grass-roots patriotism tells me to stick
> to St. Louis sewage, and if the Mississippi isn't thick
> enough to put in a bag and spread on a lawn,
> I'll sprinkle 5-10-5 when nobody's home,
> that is to say . . .
>
> it's been a long winter.

The poet goes on to observe in the second stanza that she tried to feed the birds all winter, but it took them a long time to decide that the birdfeeder wasn't dangerous. Once they fell for it, like the St. Louis grass in response to Philadelphia sewage, their response became somewhat unseemly, an overdoing, an indulgence. But who can judge grass and birds, or birds and bees? "That is to say . . . ," the poet repeats, and in the final stanza she addresses her husband:

> your life is as much a mystery to me as ever.
> The dog pretends to bite fleas out of sheer boredom,
> and not even the daffodils know if it's safe to come
> up for air in this crazy, hot-and-cold weather.

Recognitions are shy, the faintest tint of skin
that says we are opening up, is it the same
as it was last year? Who can remember that either?
That is to say,

I love you, in my dim-witted way.

Fertilizer for the grass, seeds and suet for the birds. What will foster love in the midst of marriage according to the golden mean that hides somewhere between extravagance and blight? This task of invention is especially difficult when the climate is unstable, and one cannot even remember which proportions of shyness and opening-up brought out the daffodils last year.

The same concern for due proportion and the same anxiety about extremes recur in "The Gardener to his God" *(If It Be Not I)*, prefaced by a quotation from *The Flower Grower:* "Amazing research proves simple prayer makes flowers grow many times faster, stronger, larger." The poem itself is the ironic negation of such a prayer:

I pray that the great world's flowering stay as it is,
    that larkspur and snapdragon keep to their ordinary size,
    and bleedingheart hang in its old way, and Judas tree
    stand well below oak, and old oaks color the fall sky.
For the myrtle to keep underfoot, and no rose
    to send up a swollen face, I pray simply.

In this opening stanza, Van Duyn uses careful notation of the relative size of plants in her garden to establish a visible hierarchy, a miniature great chain of being that displays what she means by order. And then she declares, "There is no disorder but the heart's."

If love were allowed to work its "gibberellic wish" on the garden (gibberellic is the metabolic acid of a certain fungus that stimulates plant growth), the snapdragons would become dragons and the bleeding heart overshadow the oaks. Shameless red would drown the delicate tints of spring and autumn, and daisies would turn into suns. The "small grace or measurable majesty" of the garden's order would be ruined. And the gardener-poet, reproaching love, likens the garden's order to the poem's order, both of which should be shielded from "love's spaciousness," chaos, and extravagance.

> For in every place but love the imagination lies
> in its limits. Even poems draw back from images
> of that one country, on top of whose lunatic stemming
> whoever finds himself there must sway and cling
> until the high cold God takes pity, and it all dies
> down, down into the great world's flowering.

Love, even married love, is by implication a rather threatening domain, like the giants' country at the top of Jack's beanstalk, precarious and disproportionate.

The vivid, unsettling color of red returns in the poem "Peony Stalks" *(If It Be Not I),* where Van Duyn once again uses the motif of her garden to represent love in general and her marriage in particular. A number of poems written during the same period gesture toward a marriage under stress, where the anger, restlessness, and mystery that color any marriage have burgeoned, grown out of proportion: too much red is bleeding, or leaking out. The imagery that opens the poem suggests both male and female genitalia, "the expense of spirit in a waste of shame." Indeed, the word "waste" sounds twice before the poem is through.

> Peony stalks come up like red asparagus,
> I said; my friend said they look like dogs' penises.
> It was something misplaced I noticed, the color of a wound,
> but she's right, it has something to do with love too in my mind.
>
> In the peony bed in spring they bloody the ground.

The excesses of love carry with them the threat of madness, abandonment, and waste. Those who are carried away by love can no longer take proper care of themselves or others, not even the very objects of their love. An example of great pathos is given in the second and third stanzas.

> Last night I was told of a woman who dug seventy worms
> daily to feed an unnested robin. One dreams
>
> of these hard salvations. Yet now the robin returns
> in the afternoon for his worms, and beats at the screens
> in the evening to get to his perch in the cellar. They are wounded,
> woman and bird are wounded. There is no end.

Too much love and nurturing, it appears, will leave the beloved unable to face the rigors of life, or even to work out a liveable balance in the give-and-take of a relationship. Thus the poet worries about all her attachments, as if there were "a leak" in her life that puts everyone at risk: the neighbor who has gone mad, her dog which has somehow been poisoned, her husband.

Addressing her husband, she sees herself mirrored in the flailing of the sick puppy: "Against intention, the feelings raise / a whole heavy self, panting and clumsy, into these / contortions. We live in waste." What she prayed not to happen in the earlier poem seems to have come to pass, perhaps because paradoxically prayer has the effect of spawning overgrowth, "lunatic stemming." And poetry can no longer offer a realm of order over against love's excess: both poet and lover, in the same person, must submit to the way in which reality sometimes engulfs us. The peony stalks come up, bright red and phallic, all wrong, but undeniably *there*.

> We live in waste. I don't know about you,
> but I live in the feelings, they direct the contortions of the day,
>
> and that is to live in waste. What we must do, we do,
> don't we, and learn, in love and art, to see
> that the peony stalks are red, and learn to say this
> in the calm voice of our famous helplessness.

Yet the poem is not merely helpless. It says it is helpless and in the saying expresses a wisdom in suffering, in unreasoned stubborn attachment. If one can make it through mud season, the red stalks of the peonies will turn into peonies. And though peonies are among the most extravagant of flowers, they have their proper place in the garden, somewhere above the bleeding heart and below the lowest branches of the oak.

## II.

Even the blowsy peony doesn't get the last word: the garden goes on to bloom and then refertilize itself by the "dying down" of flowers, the marriage survives its troubles and somehow deepens, the neighborhood persists, and the self recovers itself in self-consciousness and solitude. In the poem "End of May" *(If It Be Not I)*, Van Duyn sits in her garden sunbathing, half on view, half private, and finds a novel meaning for both the decomposition and the extravagance of nature. The spring flowers are finished ("Peony litter covers the ground"), and the neighbors who stopped by to admire their heyday have gone; now the trees are sending down their seeds, lost bits of their own substance countless enough to seem infinite.

> But under my feet as I tan
> is no longer a brick patio,
> rather a light brown
> paisley made of seed wings
> from the silver maple, which can sow
> faster than I can sew
> this fine fabric into something.
> And in the air,
> like a great snow,
> are flakes alive with purpose.

The cottonwood huffs and puffs
them everywhere.

Writing the poem, Van Duyn reveals that this lavish undoing affects her personally, as the seeds in the poem attach to the thoughtful sunbather:

On oil that sheathes me from the sun
they cling to bare parts of person.

All the long, late
day, my arms and legs are furred
with such a will to beget
I think I can almost afford
to forget it's only skin-deep.

What does it mean to be covered with little seeds, a wild multiplicity that no longer seems threatening and is instead patterned, fine, and furry?

By sending out bits of themselves, the trees are not giving themselves over to death but to new offspring, and their "will to beget" settles on the poet as she begets the poem and the beginning of the rest of her life. The end of the poem includes her observation that she has no children but at the same time brings the world in around her as the poem closes. The evidence of Van Duyn's later poems is that her life is full of poems, friends, the loud and muted pleasures of marriage, and children who have come to her indirectly and whom she has made her own through affection and poetry.

*It's too late,* I tell the tree,
you've settled on somebody seedless.
Equivocally, it nods its head.
But I have been overheard.
*Maybe for you but not for me,*
the seedy old world says.

And the seedy old world at that point is as close as her skin.

In a poem written twenty years later, "Late Loving" (*Near Changes*, 1990), the notion of extravagance comes back, almost inevitably, but this time it has its place; it resides in the kitchen and the bedroom, a circulation and not a flood.

> If in my mind I marry you every year
> it is to calm an extravagance of love
> with dousing custom, for it flames up fierce
> and wild whenever I forget that we live
> in double rooms whose temperature's controlled
> by matrimony's turned-down thermostat.
> I need the mnemonics, now that we are old,
> of oath and law in re-memorizing that.
> Our dogs are dead, our child never came true.
> I might use up, in my weak-mindedness,
> the whole human supply of warmth on you
> before I could think of others and digress.
> "Love" is finding the familiar dear.
> "In love" is to be taken by surprise.

Apparently surprise and familiarity may cohabit. That those we love may betray our expectations means they may also suddenly thrill us with their complex and mysterious density; that they may lull us sometimes into boredom means they may also charm us with their utter knownness and nearness, as "all night long we lie like crescents of Velcro."

The books that intervene in these twenty years are *Bedtime Stories* (1972) and *Letters from a Father and Other Poems* (1982). Both contain an extraordinary revaluation of Van Duyn's earlier poetic accounts of her childhood. Without simplifying or sentimentalizing their portraits in any way, Van Duyn recreates her grandmother, mother, and father, and finds her original reasons for loving them. All three were, it seems, difficult people who expressed their love cryptically and coldly; but in these poems, Van

Duyn translates the Rosetta stone that allows her to read their deep attachment and to announce her own. Her attachment is expressive where theirs is taciturn, and nuanced where theirs is knotted; but the commonality exists. I see this process as the accompaniment of a deepened understanding of marriage and procreation.

Another poem from *Near Changes*, "A Bouquet of Zinnias," expresses this deepened understanding in the language of flowers, transported from the garden to the coffee table. Van Duyn begins with the reflection, "One could not live without delicacy, but when / I think of love I think of the big, clumsy-looking / hands of my grandmother," which were, however, in the end capable of a "soft touch." Those hands lead her to the zinnias on her coffee table, tough, fresh, stubborn, persistent, and, yes, excessive. But now Van Duyn can recognize and welcome these qualities as virtues.

> So unguardedly, unthriftily
> do they open up and show themselves that subtlety,
> rarity, nuance are almost put to shame.
> Utter clarity of color, as if amidst all that
> mystery inside and outside one's own skin
> this at least were something unmistakeable,
> multiplicity of both color and form, as if
> in certain parts of our personal economy
> abundance were precious—these are their two main virtues.

The next stanza is an especially delicious catalog of their "multiplicity of both color and form," presented with the odd insight that all this zinnia-heterogeneity is harmonious: "In any careless combination they delight," and so may lend themselves to poetry. The excess of zinnias is not chaos, but an unclassy, intensified, surprisingly fecund orderliness that can redeem even the dog days of August.

The third stanza concludes with a meditation on love, love expressed in terms close to those of "Late Loving." The excesses of love are permanent but need not burn the house down or dwarf the lovers with monstrosity. Nor is love sheer excess; many aspects of love are expressed best in terms of nuance, subtlety, and delicacy. Zinnias are only one cluster in the language of flowers.

> It has been a strange month, a month of zinnias.
> As any new focus of feeling makes for the mind's
> refreshment (one of love's multitudinous uses),
> so does a rested mind manage to modify
> the innate blatancy of the heart. I have studied these blooms
> who publish the fact that nothing is tentative
> about love, have applauded their willingness to take
> love's ultimate risk of being misapprehended.
> But there are other months in the year, other levels
> of inwardness, other ways of loving. In the shade
> in my garden, leaf-sheltering lilies of the valley,
> for instance, will keep in tiny, exquisite bells
> their secret clapper. And up from my bulbs will come
> welcome Dutch irises whose transcendent blue,
> bruisable petals curve sweetly over their center.

In this stanza, Van Duyn imagines a kind of interchange and balance between the mind of the poet and the heart of the lover; such equilibrium finds its figure in the garden, constantly transformed and yet under the gardener's care truly constant throughout the four seasons of the year.

## III.

*Near Changes* includes a poem, "The Block," that takes as its theme Mrs. Thurston's neighborhood and has a sequel, "Addendum to 'The Block,'" in her latest collection, *Firefall* (1993). "The Block" is elegiac, wittily sketched out, and full of the strangeness of reality. It records the Thurstons' long-term and ongoing life in "the big brick house," surrounded by dogs and neighbors but few children. When they moved in, the block was already "middle-aged," so that the children who belonged to it had already flown, "newly married or off to college." Small children when they appeared were only transient visitors shown off to the neighbors by their grandparents.

In the poem's middle stanzas, the drama of life on the block is that of inevitable aging, disease fought off, death succumbed to. As "The years bloomed by," flowers took on the terrible function of *pompes funèbres.*

> Then bad news began to come, hushed voices passed it
> across back fences, the job of collecting for plants
> found its permanent volunteer on the block. Later
> more flowers, and one left alone in some of the houses.
> Salads and cakes and roasts criss-crossed the street.
>
> Then the long, warm, secret descent began
> and we slid along with it. "We need a last dog," I said,
> "but I can't face it." My husband became the husband
> of the widows on either side in his husbandly tasks
> of lifting and drilling for pictures and fixing faucets . . .

The children come back in a sense, but now they are gray-haired themselves and concerned for their parents, poised to relocate them to a nursing home or "apartments with elevators" and ultimately to sell the house.

The poem's ironic twist comes as the Thurstons return from a long vacation to find the flock of For Sale signs gone, a new generation suddenly installed on the block, and an invitation to a block party where "All Bikes and Trikes are Welcome" stuck in the door.

> "Oh Lord, do we have to go to all that bedlam?"
> my husband said. "Oh God, I think they eat

hot dogs or something like that," I said. Too late,
Time, in its merciless blindness, gave us children.

The poem's last word, "children," echoes and inverts its first word,
"childless": "Childless, we bought the big brick house on the block,
/ just in case." The unfulfilled wish, the absence, seems to come
back as a mocking excess.

But this is not the end of the poem; as noted above, "Addendum
to 'The Block'" is in the subsequent book, *Firefall.* The new life on
the block doesn't exclude the Thurstons or the other older neighbors, but integrates them in an unexpected way into a revised but
not alien order. And it doesn't repel, but invites Van Duyn's poetic
powers of expression to new insight, wit, and sympathy. This poem
begins and ends with babies.

"Three new babies are due all at once on the block,"
our soft-hearted widow tells us, walking her fat,
puffing poodle with a new pink bow on her ear.
"Two on the other side of the street, one here."

Within a week three front-step railings blossom
with pink or blue balloons and bold-faced signs
(commercial aids to displaying the shy new joy)
announcing that IT'S A GIRL or IT'S A BOY.

Now the blossoms are not funereal but natal, symbols that are big,
clumsy-looking, and exuberant as zinnias, and yet express something shy as lilies of the valley and irises.

New patterns arise on the sidewalks of the block: older folk out
for a stroll constantly meet up with parents and nannies and babies
in carriages, and glare or coo at the latter "as suits their hearts," since
babies mean both more trouble and more hope. Yet although this
interaction is ambivalent (how could it be otherwise, when the
zinnia-iris heart is so two-sided?), the members of the block are
truly associated. The poet invokes their deepening sense of com-

munity by recording an event designed to sweep aside that ambivalent, complexly layered way of belonging together.

> Much later a crowd chooses our street to parade
> "ABORTION KILLS BABIES," their frozen faces
> grim, their kids in strollers grim, as if we,
> the human block, were beneath reality.

As the recording angel of the neighborhood, Van Duyn closes the gates on the grim parade, and in the next two stanzas asserts the block's blooming inclusiveness and her own connection to the children who have finally, mysteriously arisen within it. The poem concludes with light-filled sky that turns into a newborn somehow both natural and angelic.

> This morning, though, the sun sends a wordless, warm
> hug to us all—children, parents, barren
> couples, frail graybeards, gays—"hello? good-bye?"
> reaching out of the newborn blue of the sky.

The embrace invoked and created by "Addendum to 'The Block'" is communal, but the poem that precedes it in *Firefall*, "For Julia Li Qiu," calls up a more personal connection between the Thurstons and a new baby, the Julia of the title. Van Duyn has written many poems about friendship and its vicissitudes and the way in which a circle of friends can function as a kind of family; her poems to Howard Nemerov, for example, reveal a poetic kinship that seems truly fraternal. Human beings are always complicating the boundaries between nature and culture; indeed, the way in which we usually signal the beginning of the blood bonds of a family is to create a new relationship by words between two people without any blood relationship: "I do."

The poem "For Julia Li Qiu" reveals that the Thurstons have taken a young Chinese couple under their wing and are acting *in loco parentis*. The father is a poet ("translator of Eliot and Pound"), and the mother is unconsciously poetic in the way she encounters an alien land; the Thurstons are drawn to them by personal affinity and by sympathy, recognizing how hard it is for the couple to face parenthood so far away from their extended family in China. Before, during, and after the event of the baby's birth, the Thurstons are standing by to offer assistance, support, and love.

In the middle of the poem, a number of stanzas invent a speech for the father during the mother's difficult labor. It is an amalgam of two voices, Van Duyn's and the poet-father's; the amalgamation of voices is not at all confusing or misleading, but rather deeply touching as a further testimony of friendship. In the father's call to his unborn daughter, one hears the most insistent motifs of Van Duyn's love poems woven into speech patterns and an elevated rhetoric not her own. The garden with its extravagant, outsized details is there, along with the double-sidedness of love, and its red flame.

> "Come to my heart, my poems. Come to this world.
> Take the gigantic bouquet the trees are bringing,
> a flaring palette of joy, take the great spendthrift
> spangle of diamond necklaces, your gift
>
> from the sky. Come, my dearest stranger, my daughter,
> find with me and your mother the metaphors
> that make us meld, come to the needy hearts
> and chill future that want your flame, to the living arts."

Read as the father's, this speech is moving; read in the same breath as Van Duyn's, it is doubly so. The father's conflation of two kinds of production (that of daughters and that of poems) may be spoken by Van Duyn as well, for her act of writing the poem is a declaration of adoptive grandparenthood, an "I do" that takes this man, woman, and child as her own.

The poem has created, and recollected, a living human link. It is a commitment to hard work and tedium, waiting and watching, engagement and calm observation, the privilege of grand-parents. The poet as well as the father can hardly believe in the reality of their acts of generation, and yet their very incredulity proves the truth:

> but, so funny, I can't believe it's true. Is it real
> (*Lili* believe, keep wanting baby, though doctors
> say don't hold too long yet) from broken water
> I hold in my arms a beautiful black-haired daughter."

The beautiful black-haired daughter/granddaughter is there, there in her mother's arms, there on the page. True creation, which summons a greater from a lesser reality, is always almost impossible to believe. And yet its imperative, breath-taking thereness compels our belief, and our belief fosters it and allows it to bloom. Thus our poems live beyond us and our children and the neighborhoods we invent by house and garden and the patterns of our life.

# My Own Private
# Van Duyn

## Sidney Burris

I had been reading Mona Van Duyn's poetry for a long time before I discovered that others had been reading it, too. This discovery should not have alarmed me, but I must confess that it did. By the time I came to her work, the poems had already been gathered together in what amounted to a fully blurbed and collected edition, and so my confessed alarm at having belatedly discovered her wide readership seems on the face of it even more curious—she was, by the time I found her, obviously a prized horse in the Atheneum stable. Obviously, that is, to all of her readers except me. I knew that she had collected her share of the national awards and grants that we reserve for a few of our poets, but I also knew that she lived in St. Louis—not Key West, not San Francisco, and, above all, not New York or Boston. And she was not—breath of fresh air!—from the South. Mona Van Duyn, I felt, was tucked away in the heartland, writing her poems largely for a few, and mainly, I guessed, for me. She was my own private Van Duyn.

I am not interested in investigating the psychopathology of my reaction to her work, although when I review the first year or so of my encounter with her poems, I do feel that I behaved—if intellection is a kind of behavior—in an unusual manner. But I also feel that her poetry is partly to blame for my unusual behavior. Why, upon finishing, for example, a relatively recent poem like "Poets in Late Winter," would I continue to believe that, even though few others would appreciate this poem, I at least would weigh in as one of its enlightened admirers? What was it about her work that caused me to overestimate my own critical abilities?

Part of my reaction has to do with Van Duyn's subject matters, and this became particularly apparent when I compared her subjects to the kinds of things that lately have been receiving a good deal of attention from exalted quarters. To take one example, in his essay entitled "The Interesting Case of Nero, Chekhov's Cognac and a Knocker," Seamus Heaney identified a tradition of twentieth-century writers who are linked together not by a common aesthetic but by the common experience of witnessing the cataclysmic atrocities of war and tyranny. "The shorthand name we have evolved for this figure," Heaney writes, "is the 'poet as witness,' and he represents poetry's solidarity with the doomed, the deprived, the victimized, the under-privileged." As for Heaney's own verse, witnessing the Irish Catholic experience in Northern Ireland certainly falls under this category, and his recent Nobel Prize would seem to indicate that poets of this stripe stand a better chance of being recognized by the Swedish committee than poets whose line of vision is circumscribed by the domestic arena. Certain subject matters, it would seem, have been earmarked for greatness, while others are destined for a kind of well-meaning obscurity. There is a great deal more to it than this simple assessment would allow—Who does the earmarking, for example, and for what reasons?—but a cursory glance through any of Van Duyn's collections reveals few, if any, whom we might reasonably recognize as "the doomed, the deprived, the victimized, the under-privileged." With so much admiration being directed toward the witnessing poets of our century, who will want to spend his time reading about poets in Missouri, of all places, in the dead of winter? When compared with the moral gravity that accompanies the work of Czeslaw Milosz—a poet who contributed to the resistance in Poland during the Second World War—how well can a poem fare whose subject concerns the travails of resisting a suburban winter in St. Louis?

In the same essay, Heaney speaks of the "immense disparity" that lies between the aesthetic objections—"nit-picking criticism," he calls it—that we might level against Wilfred Owen's "Dulce it Decorum Est" and the extraordinary human suffering that Owen experienced to bring the work into existence. For what it's worth, the poem does seem to be overwritten here and there, and yet if I were to come face to face with the poet I am certain that I would be unable to voice such an objection, not because of any lack of commitment to my own critical convictions, and not because of some incipient fear of reprisal, but because I feel strongly that the serious reader occasionally confronts a piece of writing that lies beyond the strictures of literary criticism. Or at least, literary criticism—however defined, however practiced—seems trivialized by its attempt to wrestle such a work into its tidy categories of evaluation. So I would agree with Heaney that our century has seen the rise of this peculiar animal, the "poet as witness," and that these writers bring to the table a particular sort of moral authority that much English and American verse has lately been missing.

But I would point to another implication of Heaney's argument. If the "poet as witness" stands as a kind of judgmental figure to all those poets who follow—and this is Heaney's claim —then a similar challenge is extended to the critic to develop an evaluative language that is capable of reconciling literary aesthetics and human suffering. The latter need not preclude the former; although the criteria for deciding when such preclusions have occurred remain volatile, the issues that stand behind this kind of decision making are among several that ought now to concern those of us who read and evaluate contemporary poetry. Certainly, our books, our journals, and our major prizes have all reflected this century's growing awareness of the human capacity for racial prejudice, sexual tyranny, and indiscriminate victimization. But I believe further that our attempt to develop a critical language capable of estimating the cultural significance of these works in our century—

a language that attempts, among other things, to pay homage to the enormity of the subjects that have been witnessed—has put us in danger of misplacing poetry's hold over the ephemeral, the quotidian, the morally irrelevant, the plainly unimportant. And it is my further conviction that most of the readers of this essay pass their lives within these regions.

The varied ways that we pass our lives, of course, have a lot to say about the different claims that different subject matters make on our attention as readers. If the life that Milosz has led makes my own life seem safe, protected, and privileged, then I am indebted to his work for allowing me to understand how a poem, a well-wrought articulation, arises even when safety, protection, and privilege have been compromised or destroyed. Ignoring for the moment the specific subject matters of his work, I am regularly confronted at the most fundamental level by the work's most arresting feature—that it was written at all. These features, the nearly miraculous existence of the work and the risks that accompanied its creation, account for much of the humbling admiration that results whenever we confront these witnessing poems. But it is important to note—and here I am correcting one of my own former notions—that we are not exactly earmarking certain subject matters for greatness; we are instead practicing a form of biographical criticism, a kind of secularized hagiography, if you will, when we acknowledge that the life of the author influences greatly our reception of the work. To have suffered mightily under a repressive regime and to have written poems that could have conceivably cost one one's life—the demands of survival have often snuffed out the creative spark, so whenever we find human creativity prevailing over these most hostile conditions, we are rightly humbled, often by the work itself, but as Heaney points out in the case of Owen, nearly as often by the life that gave rise to the work.

Just as it is important to recognize this humility as a form of biographical criticism, and one against which the New Critics brought such a salvaging skepticism, so it is equally important to observe that the latter half of our century has seen the dissolution of the former Soviet Union and the destruction of the Iron Curtain, and this is to name only two of the political matrices that would seem naturally to call for the evolution of a witnessing poet. In one sense, our century has received the poet it deserves. And what this poet brings to the table is not an inherently more polished, more persuasive, more artful—choose your adjective—poem than we have previously seen, but a new conjunction of formal problems for the audience. These poems live at a crossroads where the demands of aesthetics are brought into a confusing but necessary negotiation with the dire contingencies of a single life, and I do not believe that this confusion has been clarified. Yet I do believe that attempts at clarification have lately received a sizable proportion of our attention, and have in fact permeated the contemporary reading climate. Political literature, as a label, holds special prominence nowadays wherever it appears. When I read though in Van Duyn's "Poets in Late Winter" *(Firefall)* that "'the poets of Missouri hear / that their wintering-over birds are going to die," the various exigencies of the portrayed life seemed unremarkable compared with those of Wilfred Owen or Boris Pasternak or Anna Akhmatova; yet having made this observation, I recognized as well that my delight—I know of no other word to use—in the lines remained unabated, my own private delight, my own private Van Duyn.

In the face of such epic confrontations, what are we to do then with "A Bouquet of Zinnias," one of Van Duyn's poems from *Near Changes,* a poem that begins simply:

One could not live without delicacy, but when
I think of love I think of the big, clumsy-looking
hands of my grandmother, each knuckle a knob,
stiff from the time it took for hard grasping
with only my childhood's last moment for the soft touch.

There are no atrocities here, no widespread deprivation, yet the lines nonetheless are suffused with a hard-won wisdom. As the poem continues, it celebrates the essential qualities of a zinnia, a flower that has no use for "subtlety / rarity, nuance," and finds ultimately that what distinguishes it is its "utter clarity of color," a quality that makes it a flower an "aristocrat wouldn't touch." Ultimately, as the flowers fade away on the poet's table, they represent a "new focus of feeling," one in which their slapdash extravagance of color and shape suggest that "nothing is tentative / about love." But there are other lessons to be learned from other flowers; there are, as the poet phrases it, "other levels / of inwardness, other ways of loving." Here, the inward archaeology involved reveals images of the poet's grandmother and a "childhood's last moment." It is a particularly Wordsworthian moment, this conflation of innocence and natural beauty and mortality. The occasion for the poem—a bouquet of zinnias gathered in the heat of midsummer somewhere in St. Louis—belies the significance of the poem, and this has traditionally been recognized as one of the salient features of the lyric voice. To find the unexpected lesson lying in the mundane detail, to extend an ordering vision into the most shopworn aspects of daily life—such a project has long been associated with the lyricist's craft, and it is within this arena that Van Duyn plies her trade.

But this particular kind of writing seems at the moment somewhat vulnerable to the stentorian voices of political action. An entire population of people decimated in Rwanda will command, at least, a different sort of attention from us than a bouquet of flowers wilting away in St. Louis. We need not compare the moral gravity of these two events; such a comparison would necessarily entail equivocation of the worst sort, and equivocation in this matter would constitute an abomination. Furthermore, different generations define literary excellence according to their needs, and these needs, however they arise, will seek to justify themselves and ensure their satisfaction by deploying the most persuasive justificatory arguments available. In our century, the lyric voice has found a most powerful ally in the arena of human suffering—if the revelation of atrocity can be counted as one of the charges of the lyric poet, then it will require, at least, a profound lack of humility for anyone to make large claims for the passing of zinnias in St. Louis. And I am not speaking of *individual* human suffering, particularly in a liberal democracy, as the poet's newest ally; we have increasingly grown weary of psychological crises in our verse, and this I suspect is partly due to the simple fact that when placed beside the kinds of deprivations that are routinely depicted in much Eastern Bloc literature, American-style nervous breakdowns appear to be little more than a form of self-indulgent boredom. The poets of witness have had much the same salutary effect on contemporary verse that some of the radical literary theorists have had on contemporary criticism—both have insisted that we examine the assumptions of our practice and that we force these assumptions into a confrontation, of sorts, with the perceived needs of the community. Such confrontations guarantee neither the production of art nor criticism, but they do encourage honest self-examination which, in Western literature, seems a traditionally productive practice, productive enough, at least, to welcome its arrival in any generation.

Yet still I am moved by Van Duyn's dying zinnias, and as I monitor the ways in which I am moved by them, I arrive at two conclusions. First, when the phrase "levels of inwardness" occurs near the end of the poem, I realize that an entire psychology has accreted around the concept of privacy and that in most of the Western democracies privacy and the various pursuits that it allows have become one of our fundamental privileges. As a descriptive phrase, "levels of inwardness" seems about as felicitous as any phrase I know to describe what most of us have discovered within ourselves as we ponder the mysterious trivialities that clutter our lives. I am certain that if a war were raging outside of my window, I would not care as deeply about watching zinnias wilting in a vase on the living-room table; and I am equally certain that during such times the matters that occupied my attention during my private hours would change drastically, as would my entire notion of privacy. But the inwardness, if you will, that concerns Van Duyn, as well as the cultivation of it, might well be seen as one of the native fruits of a liberal democracy, and I would hasten to add that its presence in our poetry implicitly celebrates the culture that allows it to flourish. Van Duyn's celebration of zinnias amounts to a traditional celebration of inwardness that has continually concerned the lyric voice in one guise or another for centuries. Her poem is the legitimate heir of Andrew Marvell's "The Garden," where the mind annihilates the world around it "to a green thought in a green shade."

In its fundamental conception of the poetic enterprise, "The Garden" stands at a distant remove from the witnessing poetry that Heaney and other writers have located in our century, but the experience that concerns Marvell and organizes Van Duyn's poem has not yet disappeared from the spectrum of human responses that are traditionally offered up to the surrounding world. The isolated mind, continually confronting its interiority, has provided us with some of the most dramatically speculative moments in our literature. Presently, however, this interiority—what Van Duyn has called "inwardness"—runs the risk of becoming confused with self-indulgence, which brings me to my conclusion. Part of my original attraction to Van Duyn's verse had to do with my odd sense that it was being composed mainly for a few and largely for me. But by the time I came to Van Duyn's books, I had already become acclimated to the kind of poem that Heaney justifiably extols in his essay, and I had been deeply moved by the moral authority that had accompanied the lyrics that fell under Heaney's tutoring gaze. So, perhaps unexpectedly, Van Duyn's poetry delighted the very part of my reading sensibility that had fallen into disrepair under the new regime, and my pleasure in her work accordingly seemed indefensible or even, in the worst of times, illicit. But the psychological integrity of Van Duyn's "inwardness"—which, as I have indicated, might well be one of the privileges of living in a liberal democracy—is not compromised by its lack of engagement with institutional or organized oppression. In fact, the meditational privacy that her poems so deeply depend upon for their genesis and development indicates that in a suburban neighborhood in St. Louis the most egregious forms of tyranny are being held in abeyance. Perhaps such moments, free of oppression, idyllic, privileged, will always be essentially private ones. Such a fecund privacy we now take for granted in this country, and it is one of the important accomplishments of Van Duyn's work to remind us that in a free state the insouciance of one poet is no less essential than the gravity of another.

# Illness and Mona Van Duyn's Anti-Elegy

## Ann Townsend

Some of Mona Van Duyn's most dramatic and touching poems are those which examine the body in all its fascinating decay. Her poems about illness or disease often develop out of situations about which other poets might later be tempted to write elegies: the sickness and final deaths of parents; a stay in the hospital, surrounded by the noble and the dying; a mother's final words to her daughter. But Van Duyn avoids the conventional impulse to valorize and elevate her subjects when they move close to death. She intensifies, rather than transcends, the suffering of the sick or dying loved one, so that we see the body in its physicality, with its sometimes tiresome energy. Other poets write to memorialize a loved one; Van Duyn writes about that delicate moment before death. She offers a nearly clinical examination of illness from the patient's point of view in "Letters from a Father," "The Delivery," "In the Hospital for Tests," "Remedies, Maladies, Reasons," and "The Stream." She seeks to reveal what makes the survivor able to go on and, in this way, avoids the elegiac impulse in favor of a poetic that allows the body, the survivor, to speak her own last words.

Illness is a perennial source for poets; temporary maladies help us imagine death and are as close to physical transformation or transcendence as most of us ever want to get. Illness pushes us, in many ways, toward the nexus of our bodies. It indicates how our bodies will betray us, in the end, yet Van Duyn manages to reveal both the body's strengths and its frailties. Susan Sontag reminds us, "Illness is the night-side of life, a more onerous citizenship. Everyone who is born holds dual citizenship, in the kingdom of the well and in the kingdom of the sick" (Sontag 3). When we write about the "kingdom of the sick," this version of life intensified, we burn our verbal coals faster to keep up with our fevers. That, of course, is the Romantic version of illness which leads to death, the Keatsian source of passion and despair; it's how Wordsworth finds absolute beauty in the conjunction of memory and nature, when Lucy is finally "rolled round with rocks and stones and trees," stilled forever in the elegant posture of the dead. She is never more beautiful than at that moment. Wordsworth reminds us that poems about the dead must memorialize, keeping the once-healthy body of the loved one always present. In this way, language is a replacement for life, and the sick person may come to be seen as especially sensitive or supernaturally beautiful. Elegy has traditionally served us as consolation; even when we take consolation in criticism (as Auden does) rather than in homage, the impulse is to remember how we love the ones we've lost.

But Sontag counters the conventional trope of illness as a metaphor for beauty in her classic *Illness as Metaphor,* suggesting instead that our Romantic notions about illness and its consequent death are misplaced. Her point "is that illness is *not* a metaphor, and that the most truthful way of regarding illness—and the healthiest way of being ill—is one most purified of, most resistant to, metaphoric thinking" (3). Van Duyn, like Sontag, is no Romantic. She wishes to transform the memorializing poem into a record of even the most terrible and mundane of physical details, and so values the energy of illness rather than the stillness of death, though she does not avoid metaphor in order to accomplish this. Further, she tends to write about the moments before her subject passes into the nexus of elegy: she memorializes them while they are still alive. In "Letters from a Father" *(If It Be Not I),* the speaker's parents are elderly, beset with chronic disease, fatalistic about their chances for recovery, and emphatically not beautiful. The father's letters to his daughter spell out his pain, boredom, and irritation: "Prostate is bad and heart has given out, / feel bloated after supper. Have made my peace / because I am just plain done for." The mother in the poem is similarly afflicted, and the poem describes their endless complaints and maladies so fully that we may feel impatient, may even wish this couple would cease their complaints and expire. In poems that record the process of dying, the dying or dead subject is often magnified, made attractive by the poem, as here in Wordsworth's "She Was a Phantom of Delight":

> And now I see with eye serene
>
> the very pulse of the machine;
>
> a Being breathing with thoughtful breath,
>
> a Traveler between life and death;
>
> the reason firm, the temperate will,
>
> endurance, foresight, strength and skill . . .

Wordsworth sees a luminous strength in this young woman, as she wavers between life and death. Half real woman, half "apparition," she is strong, reasonable, even beautiful. The greater part of her beauty arises from her otherworldliness. Van Duyn's "Letters from a Father" presents the very antithesis of these words. In Van Duyn's world, few die happy, peaceful, or even-tempered. And certainly no one dies beautiful. In this poem about her aging parents, Van Duyn watches them leaving, piece by piece, mind by mind, the world. It is not a pretty sight.

We are taught to admire an old age that meets its deterioration head-on, cheerfully, with good grace and no complaints: "When you are old and grey and full of sleep," Yeats sings. This graceful depiction helps us accept the process of aging and dying. In many ways, we want to transform what waits for us. Conversely, in "Letters from a Father," what emerges most is the parents' obsessive need to account accurately for the aging process, to catalog every petty symptom, every bodily change, to complain voraciously about the pains of old age, as if in complaint to hold them off. Van Duyn never flinches from the mundane, even the grotesque, in this poem. She catalogs the bowels, bladders, pus, and pain:

> Ulcerated tooth keeps me awake, there is
> such pain, would have to go to the hospital to have
> it pulled or would bleed to death from the blood thinners,
> but can't leave Mother, she falls and forgets her salve
> and her tranquilizers, her ankles swell so and her bowels
> are so bad, she almost had a stoppage and sometimes
> what she passes is green as grass.

Van Duyn expertly modulates this father's voice: we hear his personality in the grip of these letters, and as in Browning's dramatic monologues, we learn too much about the subject, more, perhaps, than the father would ever wish us to know. So there's some kind of paradoxical intimacy in this portrait, due partly to the inherent intimacy of the epistolary mode itself.

As if to get too close to their misery would be contagious, the daughter in this poem can only monitor her gifts from afar, and she consoles herself in the face of their decline by making sure they have some small pleasures. She brings them a birdhouse and some seed. At first, her kind gift is treated like the medicine it is, with characteristic resentment and complaint: "We enjoyed your visit, it was nice of you to bring / the feeder but a terrible waste of your money / for that big bag of feed since we won't be living / more than a few weeks longer." But soon the parents are drawn into the life outside their windows; the father's letters sound more lively, and he discards his catalogs of pain in favor of a similarly minute description of the local bird-life. The daughter sends a book on birds, and the father's letters grow cheerful and energetic. Distracted by the birds and by his new knowledge, and with a rediscovered energy in the world, he no longer focuses obsessively on his body's decay:

> and the squirrels,
>
> you know, they are cute too, they sit tall
>
> and eat with their little hands, they eat bucketfuls.
>
> I pulled my own tooth, it didn't bleed at all.

Is this the ordinary heroism of old age? Or the easy distractibility of senility? In the last line of the poem, another, summarizing voice speaks: "So the world woos its children back for an evening kiss." We know, by poem's end, that the poet sees the darkness surrounding the parents, and the simple animal beauty that solaces them in darkness. But Van Duyn, like Sontag, believes in liberating herself and her subjects from the most glib tropes surrounding illness. Her dying parents learn how to fiercely hold on to their lives, even as they complain about them. There is beauty in the world, but also an unflinching acknowledgment of what the future inevitably holds, after the last lingering "evening kiss."

∽

The subject of family mortality is central to *Letters from a Father and Other Poems* (1982), and never more effectively rendered than in "The Stream" (also in *If It Be Not I*), where the speaker takes her nursing-home-bound mother for a last luncheon. Here, the speaker acknowledges the failure of her mother's body as well as her mind, but she discovers, too, the love embedded even in the mother's final senility. Her mother has slowly lost not only her memory but also her adult competence, and demonstrates the physical enjoyment of a three year old when eating cake and milk at lunch:

> You cleaned your soup bowl and dishes, one by one,
> and kept saying, "This is fun! This is *fun!*"
>
> The cake fell from your trembly fork, so I fed
> it to you. "Do you want mine too?" "Yes," you said,
>
> "and I'll drink your milk if you don't want it."

Van Duyn shows us the pleasure that the body still affords, in simple appetite. Again we see the strongest resistance to the elegiac impulse in an illumination of the surviving, worldly moment: life still tastes good.

When the speaker undresses her mother, we see not just the frailty of the body but also the mother's mundane and touching routine as she gets ready for bed:

> . . . Flat dugs
> like antimacassars lay on your chest, your legs
>
> and arms beetle-thin swung from the swollen belly
> (the body no more misshapen, no stranger to see,
>
> after all, at the end than at the beloved beginning).
> You chose your flowered nightgown as most becoming.
>
> You stood at the dresser, put your teeth away,
> washed your face, smoothed on Oil of Olay,
>
> then Avon night cream, then put Vicks in your nose . . .

The products named here trace the trajectory of this woman's life as a consumer, someone with "taste" and an idea about maintaining her own beauty, and also demonstrate the futility of these efforts to stave off aging, and therefore death. "Taste" is not only literal, not only the lively enjoyment of cake and milk, but also figurative, a quality of discernment. The mother still insists upon the vanities and simple habits that sustain her.

While the mother's effort to disguise physical decay is moving, what is most touching is the uncertainty the narrator experiences when her mother tells her she loves her. Is this the truth, the narrator wonders? In these lovely lines, the speaker uncovers the deeper nature of love:

> What is love? Truly I do not know.

Sometimes, perhaps, instead of a great sea,
it is a narrow stream running urgently

far below ground, held down by rocky layers,
the deeds of mother and father, helpless sooth-sayers

of how our life is to be, weighted by clay,
the dense pressure of thwarted needs, the replay

of old misreadings, by hundreds of feet of soil,
the gifts and wounds of the genes, the short or tall

shape of our possibilities, seeking
and seeking a way to the top, while above, running

and stumbling this way and that on the clueless ground,
another seeker clutches a dowsing-wand

which bends, then lifts, dips, then straightens, everywhere,
saying to the dowser, it is there, it is not there . . .

In this geological metaphor, love is subterranean, almost always
unexpressed (like spring water, it rarely comes to the surface in this
family). The daughter fruitlessly searches for the evidence of that
love. It is there, but buried deeply, and rarely emerges, and so con-
fuses the narrator when it does. Van Duyn applies a scientific trope
to strip away the layers of family history, past insults or failures, and
so learns to come to terms with her mother's death. The poem makes
art from life's insistence to struggle rather than from the more facile
Romantic attitude that death makes the subject more beautiful:

Tears stopped my voice. With a girl's grace you sat up
and, as if you'd done it lifelong, reached out to cup

my face in both your hands, and, as easily
as if you'd said it lifelong, you said, "Don't cry,

Don't cry. You'll never know how much I love you."
I kissed you and left, crying. It felt true.

In many poems about her parents, Van Duyn works to understand the chaos of love embodied in the chaos of the body. As the body decays, then fails, its workings become more visible. In the same way, Van Duyn's relationships are clarified by a similar honing; the blood ties of affection emerge along with the bad illnesses of family memory. Perhaps because of her bluntness of manner, these poems about mortality are never melodramatic, but restrained by their tight form, as if, with this subject, one must take care to find the right, the fitting, language. In "The Stream," the formal balance of the poem's couplets only intensifies its rigorous hesitation in the face of death.

∽

Cataloging "illness" and writing elegy are two different things for Van Duyn. Most often, in her poems, depicting physical decay seems to forestall the inevitable death and therefore the occasion for elegy. In "In the Hospital for Tests" *(If It Be Not I),* Van Duyn transforms the hospital into a site for a sometimes witty, sometimes terrifying assault on the body. She has a keen ear for the ironies of medical jargon, charting the indignities of scientific procedures and the callous dehumanizing of patients by the medical staff. And she explores the way in which the sick are isolated from every concern but that of the body. With morbidly close attention, the speaker notes the absurd investigations of her detective-like doctor; he's trying to figure out what makes her tick by noting "bowel movements, chickenpox, the date of one's first menstruation, / the number of pillows one sleeps on, postnasal drip," and even the fact that the arches on her feet are high. He tests her blood and urine and, as with all mystery diseases, makes her wait for the results and wonder at her own body's betrayal.

Here in the hospital the patients form a small community of

illness and, like the parents in "Letters from a Father," seem to gain perverse strength, even identity, from their bodily complaints:

> The leukemia across the hall, the throat cancer a few doors down,
> the leaky valve who has to sleep on eight pillows—
> these sit on our beds and talk of the soggy noodles
> they gave us for lunch, and the heat, and how long, how soon.
> The room stinks of my urine and our greed.
> To live, to live at all costs, that's what we want.

Van Duyn mimics the doctors' practice of nominating their patients by their disease, until the "leukemia down the hall" has no other characteristics but the disease (for instance, we don't even know this character's gender) and the will to live. As Sontag notes, cancer is "identified with death itself" (18); Van Duyn's patients have become the walking dead, with no identity in the world beyond the hospital. Van Duyn's roommate, a young woman whose husband and children anxiously cling to her, is one of these walking dead. The procedures she undergoes are invasive and terminally hopeless: "She was conscious all the time, / and could feel whatever it was, the little box, go / through her veins to the left of the chest from the right elbow." The world tightens up around this young woman until it's only sickness and oxygen and light: "the room presses in like a lung. It is empty / of every detail but her life. It is bright and deathly."

When discharged from the hospital, her symptoms dissipated but still undiagnosed, the speaker sees how hermetic communities expel the ones who no longer fit. Because illness no longer defines her in this special coterie (as it does for "the leukemia across the hall, the throat cancer . . . the leaky valve"), she takes her place in the living world while her roommate must remain behind:

> In shame I pack my bag and make my call.
> She reads a magazine while I wait for my husband.

> She doesn't speak, she is no longer my friend.
>
> . . . . . . . . . . . . . . . . . . . . . . . . .
>
> In shame I walk past the staring eyes and their reproaches
> all down the hall. I walk out on my high arches.

Like an epic traveler, she emerges from the underworld of disease to reacquire her mortal identity. She is embarrassed to be well in a place that creates identity by naming illness. We all know at the end of the poem that the other inhabitants of this ward will not be going home and that, consequently, time has stopped for them. The dead inhabit this poem, but Van Duyn moves beyond them. She doesn't hesitate to leave them behind. She chooses her life and doesn't look back.

Van Duyn's sense of irony about illness is coupled with an impatience to be well, to just get over it. In "Remedies, Maladies, Reasons" *(If It Be Not I)*, we see why. Here, the narrator traces a mother's obsession with her daughter's health. Illness has always set the speaker apart: her mother says, "Well, you're not like *them*" when she wants to join in other children's games. She seems to want to establish her daughter's "specialness" by distinguishing her from the rudely robust children of this neighborhood. In a portrait of the overprotective mother, every day

> all over again
>
> she saved me, pitted against rain, shine, cold, heat,
> hunting in my mouth each morning for a sore throat,
>
> laying a fever-seeking hand on my forehead
> after school, incanting 'Did your bowels move good?'

Illness separates this family from the others on the street; illness makes her daughter special and, perhaps most of all, is a manifestation of the mother's love. As Sontag points out, romanticizing illness is "a way of affirming the value of being more conscious, more complex psychologically. Health becomes banal, even vulgar" (26). Illness separates the patient from the mundane activities of the world. It endows her with an exclusive identity.

After the daughter escapes to college and to apparent robust health, after growing up and away from her family, the mother begins to catalog her own physical symptoms with the precision of a coroner. As in "Letters from a Father," the mother is at her worst when reveling in her own physical deterioration, but Van Duyn sees past it to the core of parental warmth inside:

> I know what she is, I know what she always was:
> a hideous machine that pumps and wheezes,
>
> suppurating, rotting, stinking, swelling,
> its valves and pipes shrieking, its fluids oozing
>
> in the open, in violent color, for students to learn
> the horror, the nausea, of being human.
>
> And yet, against all the years of vivid, never-
> varying evidence, when I look at her
>
> I see an attractive woman. And looking back,
> testing the truth of a child's long-ago look,
>
> I still see the mother I wanted, that I called to come,
> coming.

A reader doesn't often see a rationale for hypochondria in a poem; here, Van Duyn explains it as one version of a mother's love. Susan Sontag finds a similar parallel in Thomas Mann's *The Magic Mountain* when one character says, "Symptoms of disease are nothing but a disguised manifestation of the power of love; and all disease is only love transformed" (21). It may be, even, that this extreme concern with the body (the mother's concern both for herself and for her daughter) masks an equally extreme will to love and, in so doing, to survive, so she talks about herself and her symptoms until everyone knows she is alive and kicking:

> Sniffing her mucus or sweat or urine, she marvels
> anew at how "rotten" or "rank" or "sour" it smells.
>
> There's never been any other interesting news.
> Homer of her own heroic course, she rows
>
> through the long disease of living, and celebrates
> the "blood-red" throat, the yellow pus that "squirts"
>
> from a swelling, the taste, always "bitter as gall,"
> that's "belched up," the bumps that get "sore as a boil,"
> . . . . . . . . . . . . . . . . . . . . . . . . . . . . .
>           —all things that make
> her "sick as a dog" or "just a nervous wreck."

Because Van Duyn does not value illness as identity, this portrait of the mother is a mixture of ambivalence and love, its couplets both comedic and grotesque. Her purpose is not to elevate but to level, to restore her mother to the grime and sweat of the earth.

Finally, in "The Delivery" *(Firefall)*, Van Duyn explains both the impulse toward elegy and her rejection of it. The poem traces a moment much like Bishop's "In the Waiting Room," where the young girl speaker finds that "a self is being born" out of fear and shame. The mother in the poem ridicules her daughter at the dinner table for crying earlier in the day, regaling her husband with her daughter's foibles:

> "Well, you'll never guess what your crazy kid did today—
> if that wasn't the limit!" The story swells
> into ache in my stomach, then Dad's laughter and hers
> slice and tear like knives and forks and a worse
> hurt is opening in my middle; in familiar
> smells and muddle of voices, mashed potatoes,
> dimming light, hamburger, thick creamed corn,
> the milk-white chill, a self is being born.

After this parental cruelty, the young speaker envisions an apocalyptic, punishing sea where everyone she loves floats and then drowns while she alone seeks the clear, redeeming air. While she wants to save all those who surround her, to love them all, her instinct for self-survival is too strong:

> With them all, all, she is scraped by crusted rock,
> wrenched by tides untrue to heart or clock,
> fighting the undertow to shapelessness
> in smothering deeps, to what is unsufferable.
> If those she can reach go under she cannot save them—
> how could she save them? Omnipotent dark has seized them.
> She can only sink with each one as far as light
> can enter, meet drowning eyes and flesh still spangled
> with tiny gems from above (a sign of the rare
> her watered eyes never need), pointing to where,
> up, in the passionate strain, lives everything fair
> before she flails back to the loved, the illumined, air.

"How could she save them?" she asks, knowing that to save the drowning means to drown herself. It's an effective way to argue against the impulse to lose oneself in mourning. After all, she seems to say, the elegist always lives past her subject. She saves herself by leaving her parents behind. It's the living world that calls most strongly even to those who are sickest, and Van Duyn is always true to her impulse toward the living, toward her own strong and passionate speakers. In poem after poem, her characters are not reconciled to death. Instead, they grab hold of the pleasure to be taken in life; always, at the end, "the world woos its children back for an evening kiss." And in Van Duyn's world, the writer, a survivor, must always escape the dead by swimming back to the surface, "back to the loved, the illumined, air."

## Work Cited

Sontag, Susan. *Illness as Metaphor.* New York: Farrar, Straus and Giroux, 1978.

# Indicting the Messenger: Mona Van Duyn and the Poetry of Truth

Michael Bugeja

*Where so much constant news of good has been put,
both fleeting and lasting lines compel belief.*

—"Open Letter from a Constant Reader"

*Can a society thrive without truth? And if it can, will poetry die?* Not too long ago, the answers seemed to be maybe and yes. So important were these concerns that the *Georgia Review* devoted its winter 1981 issue to address them—*Poetry in a Discouraging Time: A Symposium*—asking writers and critics to analyze and respond to the situation. Perhaps more than anyone else, Hayden Carruth identified the root problem: an exploding mass media was cheapening language and undermining the impact of poetry.

> Constantly we are told that this or that commercial product or service, or even this or that candidate for office, is "better," when we know it cannot be true . . . Children today are taught, in lessons compounded every five minutes, that untruth may be uttered with impunity, even with approval. Lying has become a way of life, very nearly now *the* way of life, in our society. The average adult American of average

intelligence and average education believes almost nothing
communicated to him in language, and the disbelief has
become so ingrained that he or she does not even notice it.
*(739)*

In the fifteen years since that comment, the communications
industry has continued to explode in a media chain reaction. In
addition to the usual outlets, we are bombarded now by new talk
radio and television networks, cable and direct mail companies,
telecommunications conglomerates, and, lest we forget, e-mail and
Internet. Increasingly the media emphasizes profit via the infomer-
cial and scandal via the news, influencing society to such an extent
that millions have given up on language. As the O. J. Simpson trial
has taught us, with its high-profile lawyers and book deals, nobody
believes anybody anymore, unless there is a fee.

Through much of her career, Mona Van Duyn has docu-
mented the power of language. Like Carruth, she is concerned
about everyday lies and losses. And yet she has remained hopeful
while others have wondered whether poetry mattered anymore in
a society losing respect for myth and truth. In her 1993 lecture at
the Library of Congress, Van Duyn noted that poetry matters
again to millions of Americans, "particularly their own poetry."

Society has reached a crossroads. Pushed to the linguistic
precipice in an age of journalistic hype, people decided they could
not thrive without truth and turned to poetry—precisely, I think,
because money and mass media had not yet tainted it. As everybody
knows or learns with alacrity, you cannot earn a living as a poet;
however, as Mona Van Duyn suggests in her lecture, you *can* profit
as a person by composing poems. It is that noncommercial aspect
of poetry that more and more people are finding so appealing.

The revival is nationwide and going global. You can find poetry
in the streets again. Rappers have restored the oral tradition
—rhyming such unlikely words as "Madagascar" and "go and ask
her"—reminding us that poetry is the most human music. Rap
also has reawakened the ancient art of "performance poetry."

Serious writers have begun composing verse for the ear *and* the eye—not words on a page, but poets on a stage. One such group, "The Spoken Word," specializes in African-American verse and performs in the Washington, D.C., area, but you can find similar groups in rural towns like Athens, Ohio, where I live. Or you can go to the big cities like New York and Chicago and hear poetry again in the cafes and coffeehouses, where "poetry slams" are the rage. Aspiring poets step up to a mike and are cheered or booed by a jury of patrons. Poetry is *embarrassingly* public. You encounter it at state fairs and presidential inaugurations, even at rodeos. Cowboy poetry attracts thousands at annual readings in the Southwest. The National Cowboy Hall of Fame gives prestigious poetry awards. State library associations sponsor literary awards, too, and plan readings in conjunction with local arts councils. Poetry societies are healthier than ever, sponsoring book contests, hosting conferences, conducting seminars, and networking via newsletters. *Writer's Digest* alone reaches 300,000 each month; add to that the circulations of all other freelance writing magazines with poetry columns—*The Writer, Writer's Journal,* and *Byline,* to name a few—and you have a half million mostly closet amateurs learning the craft outside of creative writing programs. Desktop publishing has made chapbooks cheap enough to typeset and distribute via mail-merge address software. Poetry is being done at home via PC, e-mail, and modem. Major computer networks like America On Line and CompuServe feature poetry forums and "cafes." You can hear poetry on access cable or tap into it on the Internet or enjoy it with graphics via a multimedia CD-ROM.

*Why?* Why this interest in something so many in the seventies—the "disco" age, if you recall—said had died? They said television had killed poetry, and Rod McKuen eulogized it in millions of sentimental books. Why this passion for something so many in the eighties said had been forgotten, said had never been very popular in any era to begin with, said Helen Vendler had conducted the autopsy thereon in the Ivory Tower? Why this sudden renewal on the heels of such a meticulous indictment as Dana Gioia's "Can Poetry Matter?" in the *Atlantic Monthly*?

As a journalist and a poet, I think I know why. Because society cannot thrive without truth, and because media has stopped delivering it, people are turning to poetry and its various forms to preserve language. Admittedly, as Gioia notes, in a response to Van Duyn's lecture, in the spring 1995 edition of *Eclectic Literary Forum*, the current poetry revival seems largely self-indulgent: "I don't consider people concerned with their own personal effusions proof of poetry's importance to America. I consider it more evidence of our society's growing ignorance and narcissism (36)." True enough, Gioia, a former marketing executive, understands social trends as well as anyone. His literary influence, though controversial in some circles, has upheld standards while emphasizing the importance of reading widely and deeply. However, the real question here—as Mona Van Duyn correctly implies in her lecture—is the fact that thousands of admittedly unschooled and self-absorbed people are now indulging themselves, not in MTV or Sega Genesis, but in *poetry*.

Mona Van Duyn preserves language through poetry and, by extension, preserves truth. She refreshes me because she focuses relentlessly on the reality often obscured by the smoke screen of media. I discovered Van Duyn in my freshman year at Saint Peter's College in New Jersey. At the time she had published *To See, To Take* (1970), whose poems gauge the health of culture and provide insight into the human condition.

One of my favorites from that book is "The Miser" (also in *If It Be Not I*), about a person who sneaks out at night and steals people's newspapers. "Nobody misses them," states the narrator, who hoards them in her one room,

> holding my latest on my lap,
> handling them, fondling them, taking in every column.
> They are becoming more and more precious.

My delusion grows and spreads.
Lately it seems to me
as I read of murders, wars, bankruptcies, jackpot winnings,
the news is written in that perfect style
of someone speaking to the one
who knows and loves him.

When I reread "The Miser" a quarter century later, the dramatic persona seems to be hoarding newspapers almost as artifacts. They are becoming "more and more precious" because Van Duyn may realize that mass media is ready to go global during the Vietnam War and that language may be at stake. As her media miser reads about "murders, wars, bankruptcies, jackpot winnings," the character appears to foresee the sensational future of society and, deluded, mistakes the newspaper's intimate tone—which seduces to boost circulation—as the last oracle of "truth."

Van Duyn often distinguishes between the immediate power of media and the enduring power of poetry. Perhaps the book most heavily influenced by this motif is *Near Changes* (1990), whose title poem begins with this epigraph:

> from "The Year's Top Trivia,"
> *Sanford Teller Information Please Almanac,* 1979

"Bob Holt, a 20-year-old Seattle man,
was quietly walking on a downtown street,
disguised as a mallard duck,
when he was—for no apparent reason—
attacked by a husky, 6-foot-tall
bearded stranger.

. . . . . . . . . .

Holt, who was dressed as a duck
to promote a local radio station,
had no explanation for the incident.

He told police,
'I didn't speak to him.
I didn't flap my wings
or do anything like that.'"

In the poem that follows the above epigraph, Van Duyn questions the messenger again, pondering whether deep truths are being masked—literally—in the news: "Is this trivia, after all, / or a profound story?" The poet then pivots to myth and notes that gods used to guise themselves as beasts,

sometimes in mercy,
sometimes out of blind and merciless power,
but the rest of us only yearn in odd moments
of our fixed lives for the sense of it . . .

Van Duyn's poem "Near Changes" documents social changes that are so near, or close to our lives, that we no longer notice them (as Hayden Carruth maintains we no longer notice our lies). The emphasis again is on media because the poem is based on a news item about a man in a duck suit—promoting a radio station, no less—wondering why he was assaulted. Van Duyn suggests a reason: society is losing its sense of myth, yearning for it only in "odd moments" and relying not on the voices of winged gods but on ones in the airwaves.

Van Duyn depicts man in the body of beast in another poem seemingly about the loss of myth in contemporary society. Again she uses a news report as epigraph in "Last Words of Pig No. 6707" *(Near Changes),* a dramatic narrative told via the voice and viewpoint of a boar with human genes. The poem begins with a long citation from the December 8, 1986, *St. Louis Post-Dispatch:*

The pig with human genes seldom gets up. The boar, bigger-
snouted and hairier than usual, lies in his pen despite the
nudgings of a normal pig put in for company. Pig No. 6707
is unlike any other. He is a promising subject from the U.S.

Department of Agriculture's experiments transplanting human genes into farm animals . . . The main goal of these experiments has yet to be achieved. The scientists are trying to . . . create 'super animals' . . . Some side effects of the gene transfer trouble the scientists. Pig No. 6707 and some of the others in the experiments lie on their sides much of the time with their eyes closed. They are too lethargic to stand, let alone mate.

The length of the epigraph is noteworthy, as if Van Duyn is sharing her local newspaper with the reader over bacon and eggs at breakfast. But the "I" in the poem is not Van Duyn; she uses the dramatic mode to *become* the beast—using poetry the way Zeus might use a swan—enabling her to comment on society from the pig's perspective:

At least someone is with me. He swills the world,
pigpen I came to life in, and in a gushy
answer it rushes into our trough. Soap
and soup, turd and tenderloin, bone and banana,
acorn and angelcake are ground to one gulp
his gut says Bravo to. His happiness hogs our ground
as I try merely to sift the sweet from the savorless.
Someone is with me who does not need me as I
need him, who never lies alone hide-to-hide.
My snout swells out with all that might be said.
Grief, praise: one grunt, even under the brilliant
pupil of this wide blue eye of sky?

In the end, Van Duyn cannot accept this *man*-made pig whose life symbolizes cannibalistic consumption. Moreover, the creature has been stripped of language, unable to share with its companion the grief and praise of grunts. Thus, the poem concludes: "O god of the ground, I am so *heavy* with what / my tiny trotters were surely not built to bear!"

The poem immediately following "Last Words of Pig No. 6707" is, aptly, "Headlines." In it, Van Duyn states that people have lost their ability to read (hence, their language) and indicts media for promoting style over substance:

> Lines of a global banner hail us,
> tell, in words we can no longer read,
> the history of what we were.
>
> In lowercase titter, agony columns
> confide to the you, the me, that style
> alone is serious.

Media has become so powerful that it can blind poetic vision, literally in "Tears," another poem from *Near Changes*. The poet's eyes are "misbehaving" (much to the chagrin of the doctor). The narrator, who desires the mystery of art more than the clarity of science, experiences her vision returning "to normal without explanation." Rather than accept the grace of such healing, the way the sages might have via poetry and myth, contemporary society turns to media for its hollow truths:

> With brutal speed,
> this wisdom of song and story met its match,
> and science, once balked, more than made up arrears.
> "DON'T CRY IN AN OPEN WOUND," news headlines blazoned.
> "AIDS-RELATED VIRUS FOUND IN TEARS!"

In sum, the title of this poem succeeds on several levels—the poet's visual disorder and HIV teardrops—but it also implies the tears of mourning for a wiser age.

In "The Accusation," also in *Near Changes*, Van Duyn indicts media and society once more, going so far as to accuse "the earth of uncaring." The narrator states, "It has learned a lie from its grass, / which repeats itself when it's slain." The poet segues to the influence of news on people (for whom, as Hayden Carruth believes, lying has become a lifestyle):

> I charge us all with uncaring.
> We have learned a lie from the earth,
> the sweetened statistical lie
> which allows newscasters to read
> in their cheery, businesslike way,
> "In a fire ten children are dead
> and that story is certainly sad," . . .

Van Duyn invites us to challenge the lie via love, asking, "How can human love be unfearing?" The singular wisdom found throughout her poetry and expressed emphatically here is that "no lie can conceal the truth / that our kind was built to be caring."

If Carruth has identified the cause of our distrust of language, poets like Mona Van Duyn have offered a cure: poetry, whose carefully chosen words can balance the hasty ones of mass media. As early as 1959 in *Valentines to the Wide World,* in the second section of her sequence poem, "To My Godson, on His Christening" (also in *If It Be Not I*), Van Duyn looks to language to preserve truths to guide "the wordless child" into the future. In rhymed couplets, she redefines the essential words of life (including the term "words"):

> *Belong:* to swim by controlling displacement; to please
> your wavery element; the sea turtle's heavy ease.
> *Goodbye, goodbye:* that dongs in the heart; that hits
> where it's barest; said when the current of nearness quits.
> *Home:* the place we make ourselves at. *How:*
> a hook; it fishes; grapples, makes edgings toward know.
> *I love you,* spoken or heard; burns schools, unskins
> the toughest hider; wagers by guess, and wins.
> *Imagine:* a thumb on the scales; saves beefs; gives praise

at a brief dinner. *Intelligence:* prisoner's base.
*To give:* dilates the I; is a brave bombarder
of hating; is hard. *Forgive:* synonym; harder.
*Wishes:* the bones we break in the days of chums
and secrets; amended later, make patienter limbs.
*Words:* a syllabled remnant of brotherhood.
*Youth:* a green apple; secretly, bitterly good.

Over the years Mona Van Duyn may have stopped believing in "media" words, associating them with lies; but she has never stopped believing that people would return to language to safeguard their most precious truths—no matter how ignorant, narcissistic, or self-absorbed those truths may be. Indeed, Van Duyn often finds the most startling revelations in the most ordinary places, perhaps best depicted in her marvelous poem, "Open Letter from a Constant Reader" *(If It Be Not I):*

To all who carve their love on a picnic table
or scratch it on smoked glass panes of a public toilet,
I send my thanks for each plain and perfect fable
of how the three pains of the body, surfeit,

hunger, and chill (or loneliness), create
a furniture and art of their own easing.
And I bless two public sites and, like Yeats,
two private sites where the body receives its blessing.

Nothing is banal or lowly that tells us how well
the world, whose highways proffer table and toilet
as signs and occasions of comfort for belly and bowel,
can comfort the heart too, somewhere in secret.

Where so much constant news of good has been put,
both fleeting and lasting lines compel belief.

Not by talent or riches or beauty, but
by the world's grace, people have found relief

from the worst pain of the body, loneliness,
and say so with a simple heart as they sit
being relieved of one of the others. I bless
all knowledge of love, all ways of publishing it.

The last sentence of her poem summarizes both the canon and philosophy of Mona Van Duyn. As Aristotle says in *Poetics*, "Poetry is something more philosophic and important than history, since its statements are of the nature of universals, whereas those of history are singulars." Aristotle, of course, never read the *National Enquirer*. Nonetheless, as the mainstream media gravitate toward that sensational model, the news will continue to lose meaning, and poetry will continue to gain converts. May we bless or attempt to educate them.

Perhaps the best education is exposure to the canon of Mona Van Duyn.

# Metamorphosis in the Poetry of Mona Van Duyn

## Wyatt Prunty

In Mona Van Duyn's "To My Godson, on His Christening" *(If It Be Not I)* there are "the little poet's metaphors," "good only in brave approximations," and the "wordless child" who will find that the world "will hide" until "he calls its names." In Van Duyn's poetry naming moves between "a chaos of same" and "the irreplaceable thing." There are "whole zoos of wishes" and above that "the gifted air . . . of fresh possibilities," in which, in Van Duyn's hands, metamorphosis never settles into same.

In "The Vision Test" *(If It Be Not I)*, the speaker is asked her profession by a clerk who breaks into laughter when told "Poet." Only reluctantly does she let the poet "look in her box of symbols / for normal people who know where they want to go." For the clerk, the dangers of metamorphosis are at hand; the threatening eye of a poet is about to be turned loose.

Because of the denotative character of traffic symbols, the contents of the box in "The Vision Test" block as much as they reveal. But a "P-O-E-T" peering in might change this situation. Prescriptive thought is in danger, and the clerk in charge of testing eyesight senses this. Laughing at the idea that someone's "profession" could be that of a "P-O-E-T," she continues:

> "And what are we going to call the color of your hair?"
> she asks me warily. Perhaps it's turned white

> on the instant, or green is the color poets declare,
> or perhaps I've merely made her distrust her sight.
> "Up to now it's always been brown." Her pencil trembles,
> then with an almost comically obvious show
> of reluctance she lets me look in her box of symbols
> for normal people who know where they want to go.

The first thing wrong with this particular vision test is the blindness with which it is administered. Restrictiveness of vision on the part of those giving the test, that is the source of incongruity here, and laughter is the right response. If you are set on how and "where [you] want to go," then vision becomes repetitive rather than revealing. The symbols in the box have standardized meanings intended to produce standardized behavior. But a "P-O-E-T," who sees "whole zoos of wishes," threatens the enforcement of orderly traffic. For Van Duyn, the incongruity necessary for humor provides an initial step toward metamorphosis. Frequently couched in narrative and paired with her off-beat, highly original humor, Van Duyn's poems have the habit of ferreting "the irreplaceable thing" out of the "chaos of same."

"Leda" *(If It Be Not I)* begins with an epigraph from the last two lines Yeats wrote for "Leda and the Swan": "Did she put on his knowledge with his power / Before the indifferent beak could let her drop?" The answer is "Not even for a moment," as high art meets the idiomatic. After the children are born, this Leda finds she has an "openness" that Yeats's deterministic gyres never contemplated. The change that Leda's experience represents is not her children by Zeus and the ensuing shift in Western civilization alluded to by Yeats but this:

> In men's stories her life ended with his loss.
> She stiffened under the storm of his wings to a glassy shape,
> stricken and mysterious and immortal. But the fact is,
> she was not, for such an ending, abstract enough.

She tried for a while to understand what it was
that had happened, and then decided to let it drop.
She married a smaller man with a beaky nose,
and melted away in the storm of everyday life.

The meeting between Leda and Zeus has been hauled down
from the mythic-deterministic vision which Yeats needed for the
claims of his poetry to the wry and quotidian realities that, as Van
Duyn reminds us, we actually confront as our individual slices of
history. Or, put a little differently, history may be macro on the
level of mythical and marauding Zeus, but otherwise it is the
"smaller man with a beaky nose" who slips behind the wheel of
the station wagon and drives the kids to school.

Van Duyn reveals a change in perspective. The Arnoldian high
seriousness of which Yeats was so capable required its own vision
test; a revisionary Mona Van Duyn comes irreverently after. And
in her hands the grand scale is swapped for the real world's hori-
zon and ordinary optical powers, the point being that grand gestures have the half life of public announcements and headlines
while irony doesn't wear out.

Van Duyn has taken the most familiar story about Leda, her
role as Helen's mother, and introduced another change—not that
Troy fell but that the suburbs flourished. Change as we live it and
know it, Van Duyn tells us, occurs in terms of individual moments
rather than grand, historical cycles.

Then there is the second Leda poem by Van Duyn. "Leda
Reconsidered" *(If It Be Not I)* is a meditation in which at one point
the "pain of" the swan's "transformations" is described as "beautiful
or comic"; he came "to the world / with the risk of the whole self."
The conclusion to Van Duyn's either/or is that the swan's attributes
are inclusive rather than exclusive. He is "beautiful," all right, but
"comic," too, just as the transformations in Leda's understanding of
what has happened range between "beautiful" and "comic." Van
Duyn says of Leda's reconsidered encounter with the swan,

> (. . . the strangeness of the thing
> could still startle her
> into new gestures,)
> and something—a heaviness,
> as if she could bear things,
> or as if, when he fertilized her,
> he were seeding the bank she sat on,
> the earth in its aspect of
> quiescence.

Something both violent and gentle is occurring here. The poem concludes, "She waited for him so quietly that / he came on her quietly, / almost with tenderness." And when Leda touches the swan, she touches "the utter stranger." In fact the poem's final word is "stranger," but a generous preamble prepares us for this conclusion:

> To love with the whole imagination—
> she had never tried.
> Was there a form for that?

Loving "with the whole imagination" is an excellent way to summarize Van Duyn's poetry. In the Leda poems the reader is asked to follow the strange ways the mortal and immortal are joined. The ordinary and the mythical are paired; at the same time neither gives up being what it is, and the two remain for the reader to contemplate.

Leda's experience does not change the history of the Western world, as Yeats would have had it. Once the swan has dropped her from his beak she simply goes on, marrying "a smaller man . . . and melt[ing] away in the storm of everyday life." On the other hand, Van Duyn's smaller men may not be gods, but they are not without their own complexities, as in "A Time of Bees" *(If It Be Not I)* where Van Duyn's speaker rehearses her husband's labor and her own movement from annoyance to wonder. Graced by a quotation from Camus, "Love is never strong enough to find the words befitting it," the poem begins:

> All day my husband pounds on the upstairs porch.
> Screeches and grunts of wood as the wall is opened
> keep the whole house tormented. He is trying to reach
> the bees, he is after bees. This is the climax, an end
> to two summers of small operations with sprays and ladders.

What follows is a narrative summarizing two years of bees in the woodwork and the husband's obsessive efforts at their removal. Of the comings and goings of the bees, the wife says,

> Then they'd stop, the problem was solved; then they were there
>     again,
> as the feelings make themselves known again, as they beseech
> sleepers who live innocently in will and mind.

Summarizing the situation, she goes on to say, "It is no surprise to those who walk with their tigers / that the bees were back, no surprise to me."

The story continues. By November the bee problem has abated, then the following spring the on-and-off cycle of bees resumes:

> But this spring the thing began again, and his curse
> went upstairs again, and his tinkering and reasoning and pride.
>
> It is the man who takes hold. I lived from bees, but his force
> went out after bees and found them in the wall where they hid.

Having succeeded in finding them "where they hid," the husband places the remains of the bees and their hive in the garbage. Later, after a cocktail party, the speaker, her husband, and a scientist friend amble back, "flashlights in hand," to find the discarded beehive and "save / the idea of the thing, a hundred bees, if [they] can find / so many unrotted." The scientist is interested in "an enzyme in the flight-wing muscle" of the bee. "Not a bad / thing to look into," observes the speaker. Garbage opened, "the men reach in a salve / of happenings" to recover what's still living in the hive. Gearing up for this, the speaker tells us she "hate[s] the self-examined / who've killed the self." Then concentrating on the hive the men are extricating from the garbage, she describes the metamorphoses that conclude this late-night scene under flashlights:

> The dead are darker, but the others have
> moved in the ooze toward the next moment. My God
> one half-worm gets its wings right before our eyes.
> Searching fingers sort and lay bare, they need
> the idea of bees—and yet, under their touch, the craze
>
> for life gets stronger in the squirming, whitish kind.
> The men do it. Making a claim on the future, as love
> makes a claim on the future, grasping. And I, underhand,
> I feel the start, a terrible, lifelong heave
> taking direction. Unpleading, the men prod
>
> till all that grubby softness wants to give, *to give.*

Van Duyn has referred to Leda's "inmost, grubby / female center," and here the beehive is a "grubby softness" that "wants to give." A number of things are occurring. To take just one, what is essential about Leda and the beehive is presented to the reader anatomically such that there is no room for grand gestures. In fact, there is a strong element of reserve in the description of the scene, which gives resonance to the poem's conclusion.

As though they are on some late-night Kantian quest under flashlight, the men want "the idea of the thing," but it is their prodding that causes the changes the poem describes, and in this the men are doing more than they intend. There is a subtle commentary here, prefigured in the lines, in "his tinkering and reasoning and pride." One makes "a claim on the future" in ways that are different from the proud mind's seeking "the idea of the thing" or striving for control over the thing. Claims made on the future are not realized by prodding but by response: the "half-worm [that] gets its wings right before [the speaker's] eyes" does so in response to the "searching fingers" that "sort and lay bare." Matching this is the speaker's own response when, "underhand, / [she] feel[s] it start," the "lifelong heave" she experiences, "taking direction," an impulse that "wants to give, *to give*." In Van Duyn's world, results have a way of outstripping expectations.

There is the metamorphosis that accompanies the poet's power to rename, feared and acknowledged by the clerk in "The Vision Test." There is the mythical metamorphosis associated with a figure such as Leda, where Van Duyn's reading alters events. And there is the metamorphosis in volition that we see in "A Time of Bees," not for everyone in the poem but certainly for the speaker. The men may go on prodding, but the speaker's will takes new shape.

When the basis for metamorphosis in Van Duyn's poetry derives from her humor, incongruity is examined, laughed at, and by laughter transformed. In "Near Changes," for example, it is reported that "Bob Holt, a 20-year-old Seattle man" who walked "downtown . . . disguised as a mallard duck," was "attacked by a husky, 6-foot-tall / bearded stranger." The duck-man does not understand why this happened: "I didn't speak to him. / I didn't flap my wings / or do anything like that," Holt "told police" afterwards. What the reader is told is that

> With the help of paper feathers
> supplied by a local radio station,
> settling into his new shape,
> having become green-headed, rufous-breasted,
> with bold white neckring and yellow bill,
> walking quietly along,

a Seattle man began to turn avian
on a downtown street,
though the metamorphosis was only half completed
since he could not quite say later,
"I didn't quack at him,"
but could say to fact-finders, "I didn't flap my wings
or do anything like that."

And the bearded stranger?
Prescient as Leda, he sensed the presence
which to others was not apparent,
and was only protecting his nest,
the brick and concrete of Sears and service stations
where the arm that ends in four fingers
and an opposable thumb
at one touch of a button
warms and cools the vulnerable flesh
and the brain in its dear, lip-voiding box of language
and lights the concealments of space
and brings forth the cadence of cars
and Beethoven to cover
the soundless spin of the globe
whose button is beyond its reach,
lest that nest return, at the wingéd touch
of the human imagination,
which transforms past belief,
sometimes in mercy,
sometimes in blind mercilessness,
to vast and silent waters
toward whose reedy edge
Bob Holt was coasting in for a landing,
without flapping his wings.

I quote this poem at some length in part because it echoes the Ledean motif as well as "The Vision Test" with its box of symbols, here a "lip-voiding box of language." But foremost the poem demonstrates the way Van Duyn's humor serves serious purpose. "Near Changes" is the title poem to a recent volume and reveals the way some of Van Duyn's earliest concerns remain alive in her current poetry. From "To My Godson, on His Christening," "A Time of Bees," "Leda," and "Leda Reconsidered" to "The Vision Test," metamorphosis has played a major role in Van Duyn's poetry. Simply by its title, "Near Changes" reminds us of this subject, and in reading the poem we run across such familiar pairs as Leda and her bird, the tension between "the vulnerable flesh / and the brain in its dear, lip-voiding box of language," and the "wingéd touch / of the human imagination, / which transforms past belief." The tension in these pairings exists, we are told, "sometimes in mercy, / sometimes in blind mercilessness," and the habitat for all the above figures and what they might mean is the

> vast and silent waters
> toward whose reedy edge
> Bob Holt was coasting in for a landing,
> without flapping his wings.

Such waters are "vast and silent" because, in its potential, metamorphosis is vast and silent. Where might it spread next? A few months before he died, Van Duyn's long-time friend Howard Nemerov remarked to me that it seemed humans could find whatever they could imagine. Early and late, this notion, the constitutive power of the imagination, goes to the heart of Van Duyn's enterprise. Frequently humor is the vehicle, metamorphosis the result.

"Near Changes" uses a remark by Llosa, "Emerging from one's own self . . . is a way . . . of experiencing the risks of freedom." Bob Holt, the man dressed as a duck, has, however comically, made such a move, following a turn of "imagination," which Van Duyn says "transforms past belief . . . to vast and silent waters." It is to the "edge" of these waters that "Bob Holt was coasting in for a landing" when he was attacked. He was on the edge between one identity and another. "Is this trivia . . . or a profound story?" Van Duyn asks. Her humorous answer is that it is both. And metamorphosis is the event that joins the two.

☙

There are other moments of metamorphosis explored in Van Duyn's poetry. Some are more physical than others. "The Voyeur" *(If It Be Not I)* dramatizes a test of concentration between the woman undressing by the Coleman in her cabin with no curtains and the man outside in the woods staring inside, who, when the woman stares back, "slinks into the black clutter / beside the path." The metamorphosis here occurs as the tables are turned and the woman realizes that rather than feeling threatened she feels something else:

> Given her form and left to find
> its function, she'd like to see him now,
> rock at the bait of her breast
> his cheek, whose stubble
> would snag the fresh silk,
> wipe his wet mouth with her lips,
> return under his grip
> to creased, to rumpled
> thing that manhood mounts . . .

Staring out into the dark, the woman reverses the roles of the two people and transforms their natures, as her protagonist considers going "into the woods even / to claim an animal who couldn't / believe his eyes."

Another trek along the boundary between human and animal,

"Marriage, with Beasts" *(If It Be Not I),* dedicated to Van Duyn's husband, Jarvis Thurston, describes a trip to the zoo, where the speaker says she and her husband have brought their love. What follows is a rollicking catalog of the bestial types encountered, each of which shares something in common with the wife and husband who amble along in their tour past the zoo's displays. Several notions float midair: the animals are wild and caged, other and same, and they are read reflexively by the married couple, passing so many birds, monkeys, tigers, till the two sometimes glimpse something nearly human on the other side of the bars. "Nemerov sparrows" (an allusion to Nemerov's "Political Reflexion"), Jeffers' "inhuman view" (which, incidentally, only a human would recognize as "inhuman"), and Dickey's panther, all three of these drive home the idea that there are overlaps between the speaker and her husband and the animals they review, until the visit to the zoo boils down to one lion, and facing him the speaker meets more than her match. The poem continues:

> But I've lost my head, it rolls on the floor in spit
> and candy wrappers, spilling. I get it back on.
> Something, through his eye-slit, irradiates
> my bones to simmering heat. In stillness. What is it?
> No god is there. I feel nothing Ledean.
> What can it be that comes without images?
> An eye, nothing in it but what he is,
> the word, then,
>
> > after all this,
> >
> > > not love but
>
> LION?

Leda's encounter with the swan is an anthropomorphic story, finally, in myth and in the hands of moderns such as Yeats and Van Duyn. Not so with "Marriage, with Beasts"—what the speaker sees in the lion's eye is something nonanthropomorphic, a bright yellow, sharp concentration of what earlier has been alluded to as Jeffers' obsession "to arrive at the inhuman view." Here, through the bars, the alien view gazes: the eye's "slit widens. There. Illiterate. / Perfect. lion. without adjective. / lion lionlionlion it ceases / to be a word." And where word breaks off no being is. Having found some human connection with each of the animals viewed so far, the poem's speaker finds something unexpected. What she finds is "the vast and silent" potential of metamorphosis. Where will this kind of change take us, if we let it? The speaker doesn't let that happen, at least not entirely:

> but I get away, turning to where you are.
> I'm shaking. Now take what you've seen of me home, and let's
> go on with our heady life. And treat me, my pet,
> forever after as what I seem; for it seems,
> and it is, impossible for me to receive,
> under the cagey wedlock of your eyes,
> what I make it impossible for you to give.

If metamorphosis opens us to the possible, sometimes the way we understand ourselves works oppositely, determining what we, under cage and lock, are able to receive.

 ∞

"Growing Up Askew" *(If It Be Not I)* is short enough to quote it in its entirety:

> They had the Boston Bull before I was born,
> and Mother liked her far more than she liked me.
> We both had a trick. When Mother shaved one forefinger
> with the other and said, "Shame, *sha-a-me!*" Peewee
> would growl and snap most amusingly right on cue.
> I, when shamed in the same manner, would cry.
> I see my error now, but what good does it do?

The metamorphosis considered here is psychological but no less real than that seen with swan, lion, or human duck. The change is evident not in the mother's response but in the child's mind. It is the child who thinks the dog is "liked" better than she is, believing herself on the level of the *dog* or the dog to be some sort of sibling. The dog is a lighter responsibility for the mother to care for, but the child turns that into an unbalanced comparison of love. The speaker says she can "see [her] error now," which means gradually her understanding changed, though not soon enough. "What good does" realizing this now "do?" the poem concludes. The answer to this question appears elsewhere, in "Birthstones" and "Falls," for example.

"Birthstones" recounts the story of a daughter's gift from her mother. It is a ring from "some old love" of the mother's, and the mother has told her daughter, "I'll have your birthstone set in it." This done, the mother admonishes, "Don't ever lose it. The jeweler / offered to sell me half-glass, half-emerald, / but I'm giving you the real jewel." And that is what the poem is about, "the real jewel." No stone can be "half glass, half emerald," so the reader detects something erroneous that the daughter, who has "no notion what things cost," was too young to recognize. Later, however, the daughter confronted her mother with the truth, and her mother "blush[ed]," telling her "the jeweler must have lied." Of this the daughter says, "I looked in books to find out how to feel. / Then, holding them cheap, I tried an exchange of rings. / My new one tested real."

What follows is the daughter's growing trust and, out of that, her ability to see not an individual emerald but the green light for which the stone is prized in the first place:

> And on I went, and learned to recognize
> the faintest glimmer of pure green
> in a hand's clasp, or a pair of eyes,

> And out came carats of green from a guarded mine
> in grateful exchange, and back came green in turn.
> When I looked again I was grown,
>
> and my fingers were decked with rings, and still more green
> exchanges came, and we dropped them on the ground
> as our hands filled and boxes filled,
>
> and they roll and shine as far as I can see.
> Dazzled I walk the world my mother gave me,
> whose stony streets are paved with emerald.

The metamorphosis that takes place here goes by levels—from stone to color to the exchange of color with others, then back to stone again in the form of "stony streets . . . paved with emerald." With time and experience, the fake stone is transformed into "the real jewel," at least in terms of effect. This metamorphosis occurs within the daughter, modifying her experience of the outside world.

"Falls" *(Firefall)* describes the poet's formative visit to Yosemite during the trailer trip she took with her parents when she was "A gangling high school junior." This is an event Van Duyn records elsewhere; this time she describes "Yosemite's / great cliff" and the river of light flowing over it:

> The Firefall.
>
> Out of some secret opening in the sky
> the first blazing streaks began to pour
> toward earth, the rent in darkness widened and widened
> to let fall a dazzling creek, then more and more
> cascaded down the dark until a full
> river of radiance from abstemious heaven
> made its slow unbroken, quivering reach
> for whatever bed on unknown ground would be given.

Later there is a visit to Niagara Falls that describes the falls' "roar that reached beyond the senses. / No waterfall, it seemed, but earth's bringing together / of all its waters to make for that monstrous, open / . . . thunderous boasts of its own fertility." These two experiences, the firefall and Niagara, merge over time into something different from either, so that Van Duyn hears the waters say, "'Life!' Life and more life I want! Not *one* crop / but *thousands.*" The "waters' will" fills her "fleshy chambers to their core" till she is left

> Wild for the blind, helpless confinement to send me
>
> over the lip in a will-less fall, thrown
>
> from my safe, observant stand, tossed, rammed,
>
> broken, drowned perhaps—

All this, but we are told that "love alone, / however strong and skilled could build no barrel" in which to go over the falls.

Replacing the barrel over the falls is poetry, what Van Duyn calls "My field unamplified as the voice of one bird's / in the corn." Nature's wish for "not *one* crop / but *thousands*" is a fine ambition; with that in mind, Van Duyn does what she can: "I fall, rise, praise, fall, / sowing and tilling my single crop—Words. Words." Words may be Van Duyn's single crop, but they are many and they transform the world they inhabit, as demonstrated all over again by the last poem I wish to discuss.

"Letters from a Father" *(If It Be Not I)* is written in six parts, six comically idiomatic epistles addressed to a child who has presented two ailing parents with a bird feeder. The father writes the letters, and he progresses from concern about having birds close to the house, with "their diseases and turds," to cataloging the marvelous array of types attracted to his feeder. During this transition other changes take place. A bird hits the glass and is stunned; brought inside it "come[s] to life right there." The father moves from talking about his deafness and "belch[ing] all the time" to

pulling his own bad tooth and speculating on the migration and
mating habits of birds (males can have several wives, he discovers),
while the mother progresses from thinking "a scab . . . is going to
turn to a wart" to being so distracted she "forgets her laxative but
bowels move fine." The father, who in the first letter says his
"Prostrate is bad and heart has given out," that he "fell in the bath-
room / and the girl could hardly get [him] up at all," is, by the last
letter, making plans to feed the birds indefinitely:

> I am going to keep
> feeding all spring, maybe summer, you can see
> they expect it. Will need thistle seed for Goldfinch and Pine
> Siskin next winter. Some folks are going to come see us
> from Church, some bird watchers, pretty soon.
> They have birds in town but nothing to equal this.

The poem concludes with this gentle, muted, sober summary: "So
the world woos its children back for an evening kiss."

What I have always admired and would praise in particular
here is Mona Van Duyn's gift for changing things so there is more
in hand than when she began. She hands over more than she picks
up. Have the birds around the feeder distracted the parents from
their infirmities and eventual deaths or have they done something
more than that? We feel the answer is the latter, more, until the
poem's last line, which hauls us in to a much sterner take on the
subject. Yet this is done with a level of acceptance that goes beyond
any hurt experienced, the result being a new perspective, a new
slant on the subject. The change in the birds is the change in the
father is the change in our understanding of mortality. This and
the other poems discussed here are only a few examples of Mona
Van Duyn's skill with metamorphosis. All of her examples require
our admiration. They are part of her crafty love for this world.

# Mona Van Duyn's "such old premises"

## Jane Hoogestraat

In 1985, Robert von Hallberg positioned Mona Van Duyn in a group of poets who had "shown marked curiosity about the dominant American culture" and "whose flexibility and candor most deserve[d] praise" (8). He lauded Van Duyn and others (Creeley, Ashbery, Merrill, Lowell, Dorn, Robert Pinsky, James McMichael) for articulating the "range of thought and experience most central to American life" (1). Similarly, Alfred Corn praises Van Duyn for the community that she depicts: "It is a world inhabited by an enlightened middle class, and Mona Van Duyn is one of the poets helping a portion of the reading public that went against its natural grain for several decades find its way back to familiar perspectives and virtues" (48). Finally, Constance Hunting observes that middle-class privileges are celebrated in Van Duyn's work: "Her subjects are often grounded in the social occasions and preoccupations of the American middle class, a field of action by now considerably eroded" (378). Van Duyn writes an often formalist poetry from the center of American culture, and her poetry bears the mark of gender difference. She is a cultural historian, a revisionist myth maker, and a poet not at odds with the modernist traditions of poetry. She is also a poet who broadens our understanding of what we mean when we talk about the tradition of poetry written in this century by American women.

Alicia Ostriker places Van Duyn in a larger tradition of American women poets who published a first book in 1959 or within a year or so after, noting the significance of the "extraordinary tide of poetry by American women in our own time"(7). Ostriker continues, "An increasing proportion of this work is explicitly female in the sense that the writers have chosen to explore experiences central to their sex and to find forms and styles appropriate to their exploration" (7). Ostriker argues further for the aesthetic excellence of much post-1959 women's poetry: "There exists a body of poetry by women which illuminates the condition of women and therefore of humanity in an unprecedented way, and which is exciting enough as poetry, as art, not merely to be accepted into the literary mainstream but to influence the stream's course" (13). Let me be clear on this point: placing a writer in a tradition of poetry written by women does not for Ostriker (and should not ever) mean that as critics we are about to risk sacrificing aesthetic value. Van Duyn's work belongs within the traditions of women's literary history; her work also places her in the company of a relatively small number of poets from this century who should be termed major figures, the latter distinction made on the grounds of artistic excellence, whether the poetry be formalist or in free verse (and hers is both). A knowledge of the literary history of twentieth-century American poetry provides serious readers of poetry with the experience necessary to render judgments similar to Ostriker's.[1]

After Van Duyn was selected as the first American woman poet laureate, Judith Hall commented, sympathetically, "Finally, in June 1992, for some reason, the nation could accept a woman laureate: Mona Van Duyn. Why a woman?" (141). What Hall implies, although she does not say, is that Van Duyn may have been a "safe enough" choice, a woman poet sufficiently domestic because she had been, deliberately or not, misread. In her 1993 lecture at the Library of Congress, reprinted in this volume, Van Duyn explained:

> Until my last book or two I have been called in every review
> a "domestic" poet. Of course I write poems about everyday
> life—home, family, loved ones—every poet does, male or

female . . . [But] blinded by the assumption that women do not have thoughts, do not write about ideas, reviewers who are incredibly talented at understanding the most difficult and private poetry by members of their own sex announce blithely that a poem of mine about the need for form in life and art is about walking a dog, or an analysis of friendship is about shopping for groceries. *(3)*

Van Duyn cited an example of how reading for gender, as much as pretending that poets are gender-free, can be used as a way of misunderstanding a poet who is a woman.

The question of whether or when to read for gender in Van Duyn's work is further complicated by her choice to write, almost equally, in both formal and free verse. In a 1993 anthology of twentieth-century American formalist women's poetry, which includes Van Duyn, Annie Finch argues that the subjects of many of the poems in the anthology "contradict the popular assumption [in academic literary criticism] that formal poetics correspond to reactionary politics and elitist aesthetics" (1). In "Out-of-Body Concentration," Van Duyn indicates, "I confess a preference for the poem that comes to me expressing, by whatever mysterious means—the donnée of a line, a vague sense of musical pattern, a nudge of the will to collaborate appropriately with an 'idea,' or something unanalyzable—a wish to be formal" (Finch 227). While Van Duyn makes explicitly clear that she continues to write both free verse and formal poetry, she notes that formal poetry necessitates a different means of invention for the poet: "Words that he loves, but that do not readily come to mind for use, are found by rowing out after rhyme. Free verse, which draws from the island of speech, does not force this quest" (228).

Implicitly, Finch places Van Duyn among a group of contemporary women poets who are "reclaiming a formal inheritance more openly than women have done in many decades, and [whose] work demonstrates that the long tradition of women's formal poetry is evolving once again" (3). (Important emerging writers in the anthology include Elizabeth Alexander, Julia Alvarez, Suzanne J. Doyle, Suzanne Noguere, and Elizabeth Sprires; established writers include, to name a few, Rita Dove, Marilyn Hacker, Jane Kenyon, Mary Kinzie, Carolyn Kizer, Maxine Kumin, Sonia Sanchez, and May Sarton.) Finch used a dual principle of selection —she selected poems written by women, often about women's experience, and she chose only poems written in traditionally identifiable forms.

As a result, Finch's anthology has an absence also found in Van Duyn's work: for the most part, this poetry is not written in the post-1959 confessional style that characterizes the poetry of so many others who either began their careers during those years or radically changed directions then. The point is important if we are to read Van Duyn's work through the lens of gender because, as Lynn Keller and Cristanne Miller have recently pointed out, "Within the body of feminist criticism that has concerned itself with poetry, the mode of poetry receiving most attention from the 1960s through the mid-1980s was the personal lyric in the Romantic tradition" (5). While much of Van Duyn's work may appear to be autobiographical, it is not confessional: Van Duyn employs a certain authorial distance, a sense that her stories are important not because they are about her but because they are the stories shared by and happening to many people in a larger American culture.

Van Duyn masterfully includes details and glimpses from what would otherwise seem quotidian experience and, without sacrificing the individuals or the individual moments she depicts, subtly tells a larger cultural tale. Thus, her elegy entitled "Sondra" from *Firefall* (1992) praises an individual while recapturing a moment that must have repeated itself thousands of times:

> Sondra, I remember you on the outskirts
> of faculty parties, mind sheathed, immersed
> in the three children at home, leaving early

to soothe their homework, problems, pain, but first
dark eyes watching, lips in a secret smile.

(59)

For how many women in post–World War II, American culture—
for how many "faculty wives" and "executive wives"—was this
experience repeated? How often, and how little remarked on? And
in how many poems (not many I would venture to guess) is the
coexistence of child rearing and intelligence in a woman remarked
on without either a judgment on the woman or an overarching
indictment of an oppressive culture?

Von Hallberg notes that "the 1970 census showed that for the
first time more Americans lived in the suburbs than in the central
cities" (229). He does not think it accidental that Van Duyn won
the National Book Award the next year, noting, "[Richard]
Howard and the majority of the NBA committee were correct in
gauging the migration of literary taste—though they would not
have admitted doing this—toward great sympathy with suburban
subjects" (229). (Because St. Louis is surrounded by incorporated
communities and because the city prevented the annexation of the
suburbs, Van Duyn's neighborhood actually lies in the urban *and*
the suburban.) In "We Are in Your Area" (from *Firefall*) Van Duyn
plays on a tag line from telephone solicitors and transforms it into
an extended reflection that turns again to the theme of transience,
to the decline of traditional communities:

> And why have they left, the long-time friends and neighbors
> who moved many miles to country retirement homes
> or to condos in far mushroom-bulging developments
> which are hard to locate even with good directions?

(51)

Retirement homes, one notices now, do tend increasingly to be on
the edge of towns and cities, as do newly constructed middle-class

and upper-middle-class condominiums that house the aging parents (including my own) of the baby boomers. For Van Duyn, this trend cannot be resisted, and, despite their sanguine tone, the poem's lines are leading to a tragic conclusion.

To my mind, the finest example of tonal range in Van Duyn occurs in "Words for the Dumb," found in the same volume. The opening question—"And if there are no children?"—receives an initially detailed answer: "With aging, band-aids for the little cuts / and burns of friends become her steady business" (23). The poem continues with an extended, semi-comic narrative of people's, most notably Thomas Hardy's, relationship to their pets. The magnificent turn in the poem occurs when Van Duyn completes the opening conceit with "it is like, if one were to say what it is like, / what a traveler came upon, a long hot way / beyond a tiny, lonely village, somewhere / Mediterranean" and then continues with a description, in an elevated language James Merrill–like in its richness, of a weathered statue of Mary.

> Cathedral love, in the hushed greatness of gold
> and lovely tints of rainbow, kneeling down
> in illusion's flickering candlelight, may see,
> or hope to see, time itself uncrowned,
> replaced by the eternal; and the font,
> never empty of its holy store,
> may bathe the eyes that they may see the world
> as no one but the gods have seen it before.
> But here, surrounded by derision's brambles
> and weeds, a humble image that reveals
> of the priceless welling one drop only, somehow
> continues to work its own miracle, heals.
>
> *(27)*

The ending recalls the folkloric tradition by which certain, usually Catholic, icons or statues are believed to weep or bleed. The metaphor for healing is both grand ("Cathedral love") and humble ("derision's brambles"). Largely iambic pentameter lines serve Van Duyn well here; a rich, almost archaic language continues the aesthetic distance necessary for the poem to do its work. The final tear, I believe, must also recall the marvelous ending of Bishop's "The Man-Moth"—the "one tear" that is "cool as from underground springs and pure enough to drink" (15). William Logan notes, aptly, "In the beauty of their ungainliness, [Van Duyn's] poems have some of the lightness—the longing beneath the lightness—of Elizabeth Bishop's" (319).

Among contemporary women poets, Van Duyn's work is perhaps closest to that of Elizabeth Bishop and, at moments, to that of Maxine Kumin and Eleanor Wilner. Van Duyn has affinities with all three poets not only in use of subject matter and form but also in her resistance to the darker sides of American confessional poetry. Among modernists, the closest affinity is to Moore. What Van Duyn shares with all four is a willingness to work within received literary and mythological traditions and to suggest revisions that do not disown these traditions.

It is impossible not to hear Moore's relatively early poem "Marriage" behind Van Duyn's "A Definition of Marriage," particularly in the closing lines: "Announce that at least it can move / in the imperfect action, beyond the windy oratory, / of marriage, which is the politics of love" (*If It Be Not I* 35). While Van Duyn uses neither the syllabics nor the prose-like verse that Moore uses, she does employ aphorism in a similar manner. Like Moore, she is also willing to proceed by logical qualification and elaboration, and she is willing to approach her material from an indirect or skewed angle. She shares with Moore a willingness to roughen ordinary language and to draw subject matter from unlikely places. (Logan comments that Van Duyn "could make poems from table scraps and newspaper cuttings, as Auden used to do: and indeed her poems, like his, are often just intelligent talk" [318].) She differs from Moore, of course, in that marriage for her is not an abstraction. Certainly, in this poem and elsewhere, there is an ongoing, although never reductive, description of a long and satisfying marriage.

Van Duyn does not particularly distance herself from male high-modernist poets. For example, Van Duyn initially deflates pretensions in "Yeats' 'A Prayer for My Daughter'" *(Firefall),* but she does so with the end of recovery. Rather than suggesting that Yeats is wrongly turning his own daughter into an aesthetic object, Van Duyn paraphrases the poem while implicitly asserting the good will on Yeats's part found there. She abbreviates Yeats's form:

> Storm
> violates.
> Form
> generates
>
> deep
> courtesy,
> not cheap
> beauty.

*(Firefall 42–43)*

Because Yeats took so many more lines, largely pentameter, to make a very similar claim, Van Duyn's version shows a certain wry humor. But in the end, Van Duyn recapitulates Yeats's major premise: the ending of the poem modulates it to "so all's / fineborn, / let her be / poetry" (43). From early in her career, Van Duyn has shown a willingness to work within both received forms and received traditions. In the very early "Three Valentines to the Wide World" *(If It Be Not I),* Van Duyn praises poetry in the following terms: "And I've never seen anything like it for making you think / that to spend your life on such old premises is a privilege" (5).

Again, her work contrasts with that of contemporary women writers inclined to distance their work from earlier traditions, most notably the male high-modernist tradition. That is not to say that Van Duyn's eye is uncritical toward earlier mythologies. Taking on both Greek mythology and Yeats, Van Duyn writes in "Leda" *(If It Be Not I),* "In men's stories her life ended with his loss" (98). In Van Duyn's version, Leda rather enjoys returning to the quotidian, the mortal:

> She tried for a while to understand what it was
> that had happened, and then decided to let it drop.
> She married a smaller man with a beaky nose,
> and melted away in the storm of everyday life.

(98)

The mortal female here does not compete with the immortal god; in effect, she simply walks away. In the later "Leda Reconsidered," Van Duyn's revision is both more radical and less so. Here, she describes the encounter between Leda and Zeus as both human and consensual, suggesting a counter-mythology in which men and women do not stand in an adversarial stance to one another:

> She waited for him so quietly that
> he came on her quietly,
> almost with tenderness,
> not treading her.
> Her hand moved into the dense plumes
> on his breast to touch
> the utter stranger.

(166)

In both cases, the revision is away from violence or at least force in matters sexual and otherwise.

Although Van Duyn does not often revise stories from the Hebrew Scriptures, her poem about the story of Sodom and Gomorrah is significant enough to deserve a link with Eleanor

Wilner's revisionist accounts of Hebrew Scriptures, especially in
her *Sarah's Choice* and *Shekhinah*. In Van Duyn's "The Cities of
the Plain," Lot's wife retells the story.[2] The poem, I believe, reverses
the now accepted paradigm that the voice of the center excludes
the voice of the marginalized; in this poem, a voice from the center of culture speaks for those who have been marginalized by a
wrong reading of a terrible story. This remarkably gracious poem
opens with Lot's wife speaking.

> Their sex life was their own business,
> I thought, and took some of the pressure off women,
> who were treated, most of the time, as merely
> a man's way of producing another man.
> And there were plenty of the other kind—
> the two older girls got married when they wanted to.

> (229)

Of the destruction of the city, she inquires,

> Don't ask me why, for the sake of a Perfect
> Idea, of Love or of Human Community,
> . . . . . . . . . . . . . . . . . . . . . . .
> two whole cities, their fabulous bouquets
> of persons, frivolous, severe, rollicking,
> wry, witty, plain, lusty,
> provident, every single miracle of life
> on the whole plain should be exploded
> to ashes. I looked back, and that's what I saw.

> (229)

Of what happened next, Van Duyn speaks of the silences that history often imposes on women, having Lot's wife theorize:

> I stood for nameless women
> whose sense of loss is not statistical,

. . . . . . . . . . . . . . . . . . .
I was not easily shocked, but that punishment
was blasphemous, impiety
to the world as it is, things as they are.
I turned to pure mourning, which ends the personal
life, then quietly comes to its own end.
Each time the clouds came and it rained,
salt tears flowed from my whole being,
and when that testimony was over
grass began to grow on the plain.

(230)

It is terribly important in this cultural moment that poems such as this one, written from the center and not by a member of a "marginalized" group, be read and valued. Such poems, with their inclusive grace, contribute in a small way to the reforging of a more humane, or perhaps finally human, cultural center.

This effort toward a humane center informs even Van Duyn's apparently more private poems, including her description of having to stay inside during a brutal St. Louis heat wave that was dangerous for the aging. Even when she turns inward, Van Duyn acknowledges "otherness" outside of her world:

I have studied these blooms
who publish the fact that nothing is tentative
about love, have applauded their willingness to take
love's ultimate risk of being misapprehended.
But there are other months in the year, over levels
of inwardness, other ways of loving.

(*Near Changes* 54).

I don't mean to imply, when I say that Van Duyn writes from the center of the culture, that she finds all to be well there. Clearly she does not. Especially in *Near Changes*, Van Duyn acknowledges that not all is well in either the center or the margins. Reflecting on several kinds of destruction in "In Bed with a Book," Van Duyn muses:

> I lie, with my dear ones, holding a fictive umbrella,
> while around us falls the real and acid rain.
> The handle grows heavier and heavier in my hand.
> Unlike life, tomorrow night under the bedlamp
> by a quick link of thought someone will find out why,
> and the policemen and their wives and I will feel better.
>
> *(18)*

Like Yeats and Merrill, like Bishop and Kumin, Van Duyn also writes in the tradition of poets who sustain a high level of art across many years. Of poets currently writing and who are a generation or so younger than Van Duyn, no heirs apparent to her legacy come readily to mind. That is unfortunate and will no doubt eventually change. Van Duyn's legacy and her laureate status, however, widen (in part by preserving) the available range of forms available to apprentice poets. The subject matter of her work clears space for other subject positions or speaking voices, for others who might attempt to speak from a cultural center that will need to be continually reinvented to be made real. A newer generation might also follow Van Duyn's example of how, in the midst of a damaged culture, to sustain a high level of joy, as in the closing lines from "The Burning of Yellowstone":

> For two thousand miles, it appears, wind bore to the eye
> smoke from unseen deaths and wounds to remind us
> how beautiful, at the end, is the earth, the sky.
>
> *(32)*

# Notes

1. For an extended discussion of the complexities of identifying traditions of poetry written by women, see Montiefiore. Working from an explicitly feminist position, Montiefiore argues the need for both a feminist poetic and a women's tradition. But her argument acknowledges, although it is not refuted by, the following facts: not all women poets are feminist; not all poetry by women centers completely, or at all, on "women's experience"; the category of "experience" itself is contested; women writers are positioned, willingly or not, in a tradition that was historically overwhelmingly a male tradition; and subject matter is not the only criterion for assigning value in poetry.

2. For additional retellings of this story, which Van Duyn almost certainly would have been aware of, see Howard Nemerov's "Lot's Wife" (41) and "Lot Later" (263–68).

# Works Cited

Bishop, Elizabeth. *The Collected Poems.* New York: Farrar, Strauss and Giroux, 1980.

Corn, Alfred. Review of *Near Changes,* by Mona Van Duyn. *Poetry* 57 (1990): 47–50.

Finch, Annie, ed. *A Formal Feeling Comes: Poems in Form by Contemporary Women.* Brownsville, Ore.: Story Line Press, 1994.

Hall, Judith. "Strangers May Run: The Nation's First Woman Poet Laureate." *The Antioch Review* 52 (1994): 141–47.

Hunting, Constance. "Methods of Transport." Review of *Near Changes,* by Mona Van Duyn. *Parnassus Poetry in Review* 16, no. 2 (1991): 377–88.

Keller, Lynn and Cristanne Miller, eds. *Feminist Measures: Soundings in Poetry and Theory.* Ann Arbor: University of Michigan Press, 1994.

Logan, William. "Late Callings." Review of *Firefall,* by Mona Van Duyn. *Parnassus: Poetry in Review* 18, no. 2 (1993): 317–27.

Montiefiore, Jan. *Feminism and Poetry: Language, Experience, Identity in Women's Writing.* 2d ed. San Francicso: Pandora/Harper Collins, 1994.

Nemerov, Howard. *The Collected Poems of Howard Nemerov.* Chicago: University of Chicago Press, 1977.

Ostriker, Alicia. *Stealing the Language: The Emergence of Women's Poetry in America.* Boston: Beacon, 1984.

Van Duyn, Mona. *If It Be Not I: Collected Poems 1959–1982.* New York: Alfred A. Knopf, 1993.

————. *Firefall.* New York: Alfred A. Knopf, 1993.

————. *Matters of Poetry.* Washington: Library of Congress, 1993.

————. *Near Changes.* New York: Alfred A. Knopf, 1990.

————. "Out-of-Body Concentration." In *Ecstatic Occasions, Expedient Forms,* edited by David Lehmen. Macmillan, 1987. Reprinted in Finch, 227–28.

von Hallberg, Robert. *American Poetry and Culture, 1945–1980.* Cambridge: Harvard University Press, 1985.

Wilner, Eleanor. *Sarah's Choice.* Chicago: University of Chicago Press, 1989.

————. *Shekhinah.* Chicago: University of Chicago Press, 1984.

# III ∞ A Further Word

# Matters
# of Poetry

Editor's note: *Mona Van Duyn was appointed as the 1992 through 1993 Poet Laureate of the United States. The following essay is her revised text of the lecture she delivered at the Library of Congress on May 7, 1993.*

When Ted Koppel's *Nightline* TV show on poetry last summer was in preparation, the staff's first plan was to send a sound truck to St. Louis, where I live, and put me, who had just accepted the laureateship, on the show. Before they changed their format three or four times, phoning me for the names of poets for each idea ("We need an ethnic mix. Give us the name of a native American poet." "We're only using poets who live in New York. Who are the two best readers of poetry who live in New York?" etc.), I had spent some moments thinking of what I might say on the show to Mr. Koppel. "Mr. Koppel, I have watched you over the years as you challenge, manipulate, contradict, humiliate the world's leaders, the world's visible powers. Those powers are very great; they can change the world. Now you are in a new world, the world of invisible powers, the world of literature, of poem and story. These do not force their powers upon their subjects, who freely choose to submit to them. You cannot contradict, challenge, manipulate, or humiliate them. They work invisibly—they widen and deepen the human imagination; they increase empathy (without which no being is truly human); they train the emotions to employ themselves with more appropriateness and precision; they change or modify the very language in which human thought is formed. Like love, but stronger, since love's power is limited by mortality, they are holders and keepers of what Time would otherwise take away from us—the world, both the natural (its creatures, colors, shapes, textures, sounds, smells, tastes) and the social (the others we love or hate or have never known, their voices, appearances, assumptions, the inner and outer contexts of their lives). These powers, too, are very great; *they can change the self.* I wonder in a democracy (especially now that so much of the world wishes to remold itself into this form of government) if these invisible powers may not be more important than anyone ever dreamed."

∞

Something astonishing has happened in America in the last couple of decades—there are more writers than there are readers to support them. People have changed from readers to writers. I found Donald Hall quoted in the *Washington Post* last year as saying that a Roper Poll several years earlier reported that forty million Americans said they wrote poems or stories. Say that half of them—probably more, actually—write poetry; this makes a total of at least twenty million amateur and professional poets mixed together. One in every twelve or thirteen people find that writing poetry adds something to their lives, whether the poetry is published or whether it is not.

How did this happen? First, these astonishing numbers can partly be explained by the late-60s-to-80s grip of free verse on poetry and an accompanying illusion of ease in writing it. During this period, poetry was busy plucking out all its plumes—rhyme, meter, imagery, idea, traditional forms, all tenses but the present, all language but the colloquial. There appeared in print all too frequently what I called the "weather report poem," a poem that sounded like this:

I go to the window this morning.
It is raining outside
and I feel sad.

Or, in the more profound parody which I came upon recently by Joseph Parisi, the editor of *Poetry* magazine—

Here I stand
Looking out the kitchen window
And I am important.

Unable to recognize the many other qualities in *good* free verse, people felt the way open to express themselves in this form. In fact, I remember a poet, who is now well-known and has published many fine books, explaining how she began to write: she was in the beauty parlor idly reading a magazine which had a piece of free verse in it, and she thought, "Why, anybody can do that. I can do that!" She not only could do it, she could do it well, and has given her life to it.

The free verse grip on poetry was so strong during those long years that I, who had always written both free verse and formal verse, found my formal poems rebuked after my poetry readings with what in criticism is known as "the imitative fallacy"—the curious notion that the form in which a poem is written must imitate the perceived state of the world at the time a poem is written. "How can you write a formal poem when the world is so chaotic?" In fact, I confess that it was only after reading a critic of someone else, who asked in genuine horror, "How could anyone write a sestina at a time like this?" that I sat down and wrote my first sestina, in quiet defiance of this ridiculous nonsense. Though the world is still chaotic, fashions in poetry have changed, as they always do when a given form begins to seem too limiting, and it is hard now to find a new book which does not contain a sestina or two. During the period preceding the fashion of free verse, when much American poetry was rhymed, metered, and dense with imagery, it was easier for non-poets to tell the difference between naive attempts at poetry by people who saw only one aspect of it and felt they could write it and the genuine poem.

Other factors probably contributed to the gigantic increase in writing poetry. About twenty years ago the "poets in the schools" emissaries began their work of teaching youngsters to write poems. Somewhat later poetry therapy caught fire, with its emissaries working in prisons, hospitals, mental institutions, and nursing homes. Therapy poetry, by the way, uses the poem to validate the self; professional poets use the self to validate and reanimate the art. (So far as I am concerned, both have value, if not equal value.)

Where are all these people who are writing poetry? They are everywhere, very visible in America. Dana Gioia, whose controversial article "Can Poetry Matter?" in the *Atlantic Monthly* in 1991 (which later became the title essay of his book) was a curious mixture of profound truth and totally unsound speculation, ignorance, and unsupported assumption, asserts that all the professional and would-be professional writers are in the academies and, seemingly, in his view, are remaining there, though how the universities could hold them all without exploding their walls I would not know. As a result, he feels, poetry has withdrawn from "mainstream culture," of which only a short time ago it was an integral part, and that everyone is writing "academic" poetry. As Philip Levine, whose poems focus primarily on working-class experience, says in a 1992 interview, "There's a myth that just yesterday there were millions reading poetry and suddenly somehow . . . they all turned to fiction or to the movies or something. I think that's nonsense . . . How many people read [past tense] Keats? How many people were reading Emily Dickinson? If I want to be read by hundreds of thousands of people I better get a job with *Reader's Digest* and write bullshit."

My experience at teaching graduate poetry writing workshops demonstrated that students bring a wide variety of backgrounds and experiences, as well as a wide variety of relationships to the poetry of the past, to their poems. There is no standard workshop poem, academic or otherwise. Anne Sexton's self-enclosed confessional poetry and Maxine Kumin's outward-looking poems about country life came out of the same workshop. Students come to learn, through feedback from fellow students, how better to make their poems communicate to readers, to have the teaching poet point out, protect, and help develop what is original in their work. Then they go out to earn their living and support their families by working with computers, starting up PR agencies, ghostwriting and editing, teaching in high school, writing greeting-card verse for Hallmark, forming house-painting and repair groups—whatever they can find to do that will give them time to write their poetry.

And the writing of poetry can be seen at summer workshops: so many hundreds of people flock to them on so many campuses that more and more universities, hearing that they can help their deficits by using their facilities, otherwise half-vacant during the summer months, are starting such programs. I have taught in them in four parts of the country. These students range in age from late teens to late eighties, with corresponding differences in experiences. Then there are the sixty or more Poets' Houses and Writers' Places in cities all over the country, filled with tapes and books of poetry, serving as centers in which professional poets, amateur poets, and people simply interested in poetry can meet. And there are the innumerable poetry readings, by means of which certain non-teaching poets (myself among them) make their living, in every city and town in every state. I counted seven poetry readings in one randomly selected month in the St. Louis "Calendar of Events." There are university readings, YWHA and YMCA readings, civic readings, coffeehouse and bar and restaurant readings, state-wide poetry festival readings, readings at all summer writing programs, open microphone readings, readings at high-school and university commencements, readings at all the Poets' Houses and Writers' Places earlier mentioned. Over the years there has been a steady increase in the size of the audiences. Larger and larger theaters and halls are filled, whether the readings are free or require a fee. Poets are very visible and audible all over America.

∞

At the same time, sales of poetry books by the same poets who read are down, editors report. The expenses-paid fee for one reading often pays more than the year's income from one of the poet's books, and many of us give ten or twenty readings a year. Television seems an obvious culprit, leading people to wish to see the poet and watch his/her lips move as they hear the poems. One might think that poetry was happily returning to its oral pre-printing-press form, but since it is a frequently noted fact that memory cannot preserve free verse at all, and is obviously incapable of preserving the vast quantities of rhymed and metered verse becoming available once more, there seems a necessity for printed preservation. Books must be printed; to be printed, they must be sold. Libraries do their best to follow their reviewing guides and acquire what seems the best poetry being published, but cannot, of course, invest in anywhere near all of it. The cost of a book of poems has risen, but so has the cost of all other books, CDs, videos, concert tickets, theater tickets, and the many other cultural things that people freely spend their money on. People simply prefer to write it and hear it read, particularly to write it, than to buy and read it. Instead of asking, "Can poetry matter?" Mr. Gioia might better address himself to the question of why, in America, poetry matters so much to so many people, particularly their own poetry.

I can speculate about why so many millions of people in America wish to write poetry or to be poets, but this is speculation only. We live in a mass culture whose attitude and philosophy are commercial. Its aim in far too many things is to make the greatest profit by producing for the average and by changing fashions in everything in order to force masses of people to keep buying new things. Individuals are compressed, homogenized into gigantic groups: voters, consumers, teens, Yuppies, senior citizens, ethnics, Wasps, etcetera. Everything from TV programs to shoe sizes are produced for only the greatest number. When fashionable colors and textures change to stimulate sales (for clothing, for redecoration of the house, from carpets and refrigerators to bathtowels), certain colors and styles are "in" and others simply unavailable. No self wishes to be medium, no self *is* average, no self wishes to dress or decorate a home in colors and textures dictated by commerce. Instead of living with others like a leaf on a tree which is seen only as a leafy mass, each self wishes to live in a world that illustrates the title of Rosanna Warren's book of poems, *Each Leaf Shines Separate.*

Expression of the self in amateur poetry is an attempt to validate the self and its perceptions, its inmost feelings and thoughts. People to my own knowledge who write it include a chambermaid, a nursing home inmate, a grandmother, a psychiatrist, a Milton scholar, a mortician, a man dying of cancer, a businessman, a librarian, a nun, an adolescent, a farmer, a professional baseball player.

For what other reasons do nonprofessionals write poetry? Many of those who seek help in workshops in order to get published have a dream, I think, not so much of devoting the most intense part of their lives to the hard, lonely, glorious, transcendent play-work of writing poetry, but of appearing before the world as a poet. It is a dream of individual freedom, an unexamined, perhaps even unconscious need in a country where even the individualizing first name of a human being has been reduced to the uniformed and meaningless: "My name is Jean; I am your waitress for the evening." It does not in any way resemble the hippie rebellion in which youth divided itself from age by dressing alike, acting, talking, wearing their hair, eating, living alike. The point of this dream is the expression of the freedom and uniqueness of a self. Need I say that, though some few professional poets have indeed felt free to express outwardly their quirky selfness, it is the strong inner sense of self, usually protected from the public eye, saved from and dedicated to the poems, that is characteristic of most successful publishing poets? Most of them are happy to be indistinguishable in public, leading quiet, domestic lives. The private aspects of the wild and unique are saved for the poems. Iconoclasm is saved, hoarded, for language—for forms on the page.

∞

Out of the millions of Americans who write some sort of poetry have risen the successful, talented, dedicated, book-publishing poets. Never before in the history of this country have there been so many of those. Twenty or so years ago, there were approximately thirty major poets, whose work I kept up with, priding myself on my ability to do so; now there are hundreds, and no one person could conceivably read all their work as it comes out.

The latest edition of *Poets and Writers* lists more than 4,000 poets who are available for readings, and some poets do not wish to be so listed. *Poetry* magazine receives between 900 and 1,000 books of poems a year for review. These are poets who must have a book-buying audience. First-book publication contests (of poetry organizations, university presses, and private publishers), of which I have judged over a dozen, may have one or two thousand entries (to be weeded out by sub-judges before they read the thirty or so manuscripts that come to the final judge). The major national contests have so many candidates for the best book or poet in the nation for that year that the judges are almost overwhelmed by the job of reading, and some of them are tempted simply to give a prize to the poet who has already won the most prizes, since he must be the best—or so it sometimes seems. The Lenore Marshall–*Nation* prize, whose panel of three judges I chaired and to which the publishers sent their "best bets," had 200 entries in 1992. For the Bollingen recently, each of us three judges was asked to submit a list of ten candidates before the meeting, a list of ten poets who were worthy of the prize and had not won it before in all its years of operation. There was not a single duplication of name on the three lists, making a total of thirty poets worthy of one of America's three top prizes (the others being the National Book Award and the Pulitzer Prize)—that is, one part of what is called the Triple Crown.

Side by side with this explosion in number and excellence in professional American poets, more and bigger prizes are being awarded each year. Besides the Guggenheim grants, the Triple Crown prizes, the troubled NEA grants, the many poetry prizes awarded by the American Academy of Arts and Letters, and the Academy of American Poets Fellowship, there are the lavish MacArthur Fellowships of hundreds of thousands of dollars per person. The new Ruth Lilly *Poetry* Magazine Prize had hardly become known as the largest yearly prize ($30,000) when it was topped by a $40,000 prize, quickly followed last year by a $50,000 one. The Ruth Lilly Foundation has just announced that its *Poetry* Magazine Prize will be $75,000 this year. The Academy of American Poets felt called upon to offer one $20,000 fellowship each year instead of two $10,000 ones, which seemed too puny. The state and national governments, industries, foundations, and many private donors seem to be vying with each other to shower money on poets. (How can poetry "matter" so much to so many donors? one might ask Mr. Gioia.)

To meet the explosion in number of professional, publishing poets, literary magazines have co-exploded in number. There were only nine or ten when, in 1947, my husband and I began publishing and paying for our magazine, *Perspective*. Now, I suppose, there must be well over a thousand, from stately journals paid for by a university to the deliberately antistately "littles" with names like *Fuckyou, Horsetail, Broomstraw, Howling Dog, Loonfeather.* They are supported by state and federal grants, private donors, and their own editors. University presses, in the late '50s and early '60s, began publishing poetry alongside their scholarly publications. Commercial presses expanded their poetry lists (Knopf now publishes all the books of forty poets), although poetry is a prestige item, not a moneymaker.

Besides the flood of Wasp poetry there was the fairly recent enrichment of Afro-American poetry, and the even more recent upsurge in the printing of poetry books by women. The women's movement created inescapable pressure on publishers to add at least a token woman to their lists. In the '50s and '60s it was extremely hard for a woman to get a book published at all. The first effect of the women's movement was the move of the university presses to publish anthologies of women's poetry, thus displaying the range and number of women who were writing professionally. This ghettoization of women poets was not entirely pleasant, and as time went on, more and more editors broke down and added talented women poets to their lists, and more and more women poetry editors were hired. Although it seems almost unbelievable, for twenty years I was the only woman on one publisher's list of twenty poets, accepted only because three of the male poets had strongly recommended me. My first book with this commercial press won the National Book Award. Now, his consciousness having risen along with those of many other editors of poetry at other presses, my editor publishes many women with great enthusiasm and pride.

The most recent rainstorm that has nearly flooded the banks of the river of poetry being published is American ethnic poetry. Publishers have found both prestige and grant money ready and willing to invest in publishing Eskimo poets, Hispanic poets, Chinese poets, Native American poets, and so on. To this is added a rage for translation of poetry from countries as yet untapped for this purpose, as well as for poetry in languages difficult to translate. So the number of poetry books published each year is raised still higher by translations from the Russian and Chinese, as well as Bulgarian (two anthologies in one year), Catalan, Korean, Serbian. And of course we have our distinguished émigré poets, among them Brodsky and Milosz. Naturally the translation of European poets continues, as well as the republication here of the poets of England, Scotland, Ireland, and Wales.

How are all these books of poetry going to reach the audience that does exist (an audience outside of the other professional poets, who are aware of the existence of these books but no one of whom could afford to buy them all)? How is that general audience (and, as I will explain, no one knows how large it is or could be) to know which books are the best books or, which is perhaps more important, which ones they would most enjoy owning or reading? Some poets are more accessible than others to an inexperienced reader, some have qualities that appeal to some people but not to others. On a one-hour call-in radio show I was asked, "*New Yorker* poetry doesn't speak to me. Where are poets who are easier to read?" This man, not being all that interested, obviously would not search through every issue to find, among the many kinds of poems the *New Yorker* prints, a poet he might like; he needs critical guidance. Another caller asked, "Why can't we have rhyme any more? I like rhymed poetry." He doesn't know that rhyme and meter are back "in style" and once more exist in abundance in very recent poetry. How could he know? *There is no way to tell the public anything about poetry.*

One might think that poetry readings would be one very effective way to reach the public with books they know they would enjoy, and indeed it is when the reader's books are conveniently on sale at the reading. But that happy collocation of reader, audience, and books is not the general rule at a reading. The small or large amount of newspaper publicity that accompanies the awarding of the national prizes is another way. The Pulitzer, actually, is the only one that a large general public hears about. Since it is largely a series of prizes for journalists, every newspaper in the country is in the running for its prizes and announces all the winners; the few literary winners ride in on the nationwide publicity given the many journalistic winners.

This leaves, as a way of making books of poems or poets known to a wide audience, publicity paid for by publishers, who cannot afford it, and published critical comment which will describe the books adequately and discriminatingly so that both writers and general audience will know which are good, which bad, and so that members of the general audience may find what they like. I must add here that when, by some means or other, members of the public wish to buy a certain book of poems, they are nearly always unable to do so. Bookstores cannot afford to take up so much of their shelf space with so many slow-moving books. All of us traveling poets know the frustration of being asked in a strange city, "Where can I buy your book here?" We do not know—probably nowhere. For the admirer to go to all the trouble of ordering the book from the publisher takes weeks; few people are that devoted and determined.

⚭

So poetry desperately needs criticism, as both discrimination and publicity, to reach an audience. There are three kinds of critics: anthologists, who decide which poets will reach people in high schools and colleges or universities and, in effect, make up the canon of what poets should be preserved for the ages; reviewers for newspapers; and critics in literary journals and books.

Let's take a look at the anthologies first. Are they doing their job of preserving American poetry? Not unless one assumes that the public will find little of interest in poetry by women. Out of curiosity some ten years ago, I counted poets in ten anthologies whose publication dates began in 1960 and ran to 1980. Recently I added a fine anthology published in 1990. Before I give the results, which I think will surprise you, I wish to point out that around 1960 there were fifty-some good, publishing women poets; now, of course, there are hundreds. Here are the figures:

|      | MEN | WOMEN |
|------|-----|-------|
| 1962 | 23  | 2     |
| 1964 | 30  | 3     |
| 1965 | 51  | 8     |
| 1968 | 17  | 2     |

| 1969 | 23 | 8 |
| 1970 | 39 | 5 |
| 1973 | 14 | 15 |
| 1977 | 39 | 11 |
| 1979 | 166 | 59 |
| 1980 | 33 | 7 |
| 1990 | 48 | 16 |

Among the leading American women poets there are four especially striking omissions from the large and popular anthology which contains 141 men and 15 women. These four women hold among them the following honors (to keep them anonymous I will simply make a group list): three Library of Congress poetry consultantships, an Academy of American Poets Fellowship, two Chancellorships of the Academy of American Poets, three Pulitzer Prizes, a Bollingen Prize, a National Book Award, and too many other smaller prizes and fellowships to mention.

∞

I think these few simple statistics make the case for the lack of generosity in offering the public a chance to like poetry by women on the part of the male-dominated poetry world better than any harangue I might be tempted to make. What has been happening is undesirable. When I spoke of this in 1991 to a very sympathetic, very un-macho male literary friend, I mentioned the omission of a distinguished female poet from the 1990 anthology. He said instantly, "But she's not a great poet." I mentioned the name of one male poet in the anthology and asked if he was a great poet. "Of course not—far from it—good, yes." I mentioned another man included. Same answer. Another. "Well," my friend said, "I guess you're perfectly right." What I am right about is that women have to be seen as great poets to be included in anthologies, men need only be good poets. So even that segment of the general public which is exposed to anthologies is denied a sample of the poetry of many women whom they might enjoy and whose books they might buy.

The second and third possibilities of reaching a public are the reviews in the newspapers, read by both the poets' peers and the public (these are printed when the book comes out); and the longer, more thoughtful, later criticism in magazines and literary journals. Alas! At the same time that books of poetry began seriously to proliferate, these slender means of reaching a receptive public that exists or might exist began closing down and continued drastically to decrease as the poetry continued to increase.

∞

The *New York Times Book Review,* which formerly had a poetry editor and where worthy books of poems were regularly discussed at length, dropped this category of reviewing almost entirely. In a fifty-two-issue year, poetry is reviewed about four to six times. When it is reviewed, it is given one page, on which three books must be dealt with briefly.

From the publication of my second book in 1964 through 1983, each of my books had received at least twenty newspaper reviews, besides the magazine reviews. Between 1982, when my sixth book was published, and 1990, when the seventh came out, a startling decrease in newspaper reviewing of poetry took place, catching me by complete surprise. When I received only four newspaper reviews, none from San Francisco, Houston (where I used to be reviewed in two newspapers), Washington, D.C., Chicago, cities in the South, places that had always reviewed me, I accused my publishers of failing to send review copies. They sent me computer sheets showing that they had sent hundreds of them. Something had happened, and to newspapers, not to my book, which later won the Pulitzer.

Newspapers used to have a steady in-town poet-reviewer of poetry and a small stable of out-of-town, perhaps more prestigious, reviewers for particularly prestigious poets. Some poets, fortunately, are willing to do the work of reviewing, since one of the well-known ways of poking one's head above the mob of fellow poets is to become a reviewer. Sadly, many poets have begun to notice that the reviews were ceasing to describe, discriminate, and criticize, and were turning into mere blurbs for the books. (Here I agree with Mr. Gioia.) Gone was any wholesome, necessary, honest discrimination between the good and the bad like Jarrell's criticism, which among other things single-handedly saved Whitman as a major poet by excoriating his embarrassingly bad parts and pointing out the beautiful passages. Who has not read the gorgeous, inflated rhetoric of praise in a review and then suddenly burst into laughter at the quoted passage the critic has been talking about, the bad, flat, inept lines that provoked that incandescent praise? Poets who happily are still willing to be reviewers for the reward of being wooed by their peers to get a review must, unhappily, always praise, for nasty may be the revenge on the reputation of their own poetry if they are truthful about what is bad in others. So the bad books, the weak books, are given the same public weight as the astonishingly good ones, the near-great ones. The public has not been helped to find a good book nor even one, good or bad, that it might like.

The dropping of reviews from newspapers has several causes. Newspapers in general are in deep financial trouble, with TV, the principal villain, having taken away their big business advertising and cut down on their circulation, because so many people are content with the condensed show-and-tell version of TV news and sports. Newspapers, which have never sent a reviewer to a poetry reading, no matter how prestigious the performer (with the exception of Pittsburgh, where a reading is reviewed the next morning by two newspapers), though they consistently send knowledgeable reviewers to the tiny local art openings and musical events, can no longer even support an adequate weekend book-page. Poetry is the first to go. Also, the increase in number of poetry books has itself helped eliminate the newspaper reviewing of it. When book-page editors are so inundated by poetry books, I have heard some of them say that neither they nor their ill-paid poetry reviewer has time or knowledge to decide which few to choose for review. It's simpler to eliminate poetry reviewing altogether.

Something even more drastic took place a number of years ago to the National Book Award. Publishers, who paid for the lavish dinners, the renting of Alice Tully Hall for the ceremonies, the congratulatory ads in newspapers to their winners, complained that all this was not paying off in increased sales of the winning books in all categories of literature. They first began an attempt to make the awards into a Hollywood Oscar–type razzle-dazzle on TV, then, when that comically failed, reduced categories such as book design, first book, etcetera. Poetry, and poetry alone, was completely removed from the category of literature; it ceased to be thought of by the National Book Award as a kind of book. Three years ago the publishing cadre allowed poetry to re-enter literature.

The journals and "little magazines" that publish thoughtful, later reviews are all inundated by books also. *Poetry* magazine, which can review perhaps fifty books in its twelve yearly issues, struggles with its thousand submissions for review a year. When I was reading in California, the poet-critic in whose house I was staying was preparing to do a review for *Poetry.* He showed me a list of sixty or more new books, an already weeded out selection by the editor, from which he was to choose the four or five for one monthly review. "I don't know these poets," he said. "Can you tell me which ones you think I might find interesting?" Since I had judged so many contests, I knew about two-thirds of their names and the work and was able to make some suggestions. But I saw vividly and firsthand the problem I've been discussing.

It is in the literary journals which still review for literary readers that the competitive pressure of so many publishing poets is becoming truly nasty. I will try to keep everything anonymous in touching on this subject. One poet laureate and presidential gold medalist published a book which did not receive a single review anywhere; another of his books was given a terrible review and, after that was published, another magazine employed the same reviewer to review it again, knowing the same thing would happen. One of America's most brilliant poets, one whom one would give one's non-writing arm to equal, was called by an influential poetry critic "a phony poet." A concerted attempt to destroy two others of America's top older poets also took place fairly recently. Laureate X, whose poetry has an almost religious reverence for and tenderness toward all living things, was called in a literary magazine a Fascist, a racist, a misogynist, and an elitist. When he wrote the magazine asking if he might write a rebuttal, he was told he could do so only if the reviewer of his life's work could have the last word in a rebuttal of the rebuttal. Top American poet Y, who often writes difficult poetry but also writes narrative poetry of luminous clarity, had one of his narratives, whose "story" an intelligent ten-year-old could grasp, distorted in a summary in five major ways and its conclusion grotesquely misinterpreted so that the reviewer could charge him with being a racist. Another absurd attack on him is too long to summarize here, but the "proof" offered by a young reviewer that his major work is meaningless is so absurd and so easily countered by one obvious fact that one can hardly believe an editor would allow such malicious nonsense in his magazine. Seemingly, since these older poets are still writing vigorously and well and have not, like ancient, sick Eskimos, voluntarily walked away from burdening the family to freeze to death on the ice, the only option for the younger ones is to try to slaughter them. This kind of pressure from below to get the great major poets out of the way so younger ones can assume a top position is the only really repulsive aspect of the otherwise harmless explosion of publishing poets who can't find a book-buying audience.

It is in the journal reviews also that women poets are kept firmly in their place. They may be given good reviews, but there are other ways of holding women back from a full appreciation of their art. The most blatant discrimination I have seen recently was in the reviewing of two books which came out close together, one by a distinguished older woman poet, one by a still older distinguished male poet. The books were remarkably similar in their authors' passion for life, their continuing appreciation of the opposite sex, their humor, and their ironic but open-eyed awareness of their own mortality. One review of the woman's book saw these aspects of the book and labeled it "an old woman's book." The reviewer of the man's book compared it rapturously and at length to the beautiful, passionate poems of the late Yeats, which, of course, are among the most gorgeous poems of old age in our language.

But usually the discrimination is not so blatant. Here I will drop the use of anonymity and use myself simply as an example. Until my last book or two I have been called in every review a "domestic" poet. Of course I write poems about everyday life—home, family, loved ones—every poet does, male or female. But ever since high school I have enjoyed writing extended metaphor poems, writing about one thing in terms of another, which gives me a chance to play with the double meanings of words which can work simultaneously on both sides of the metaphor. A short introductory poem in one of my books, about how art and love can preserve what Time would otherwise take away, uses as a metaphor for writing my sweet-and-sour poems the canning of pickled peaches, and I compare myself humbly to Proust, who preserved the past so beautifully in his art. Male reviewers insist that the poem is about canning peaches. Blinded by the assumption that women do not have thoughts, do not write about ideas, reviewers who are incredibly talented at understanding the most difficult and private poetry by members of their own sex announce blithely that a poem of mine about the need for form in life and art is about walking a dog, or an analysis of friendship is about shopping for groceries.

⌒

So what are we going to do about the facts that one in every twelve or thirteen people in this country takes pleasure in writing poetry; that people by the several thousands have written books of poems they wish to get published and seriously intend to become professional poets; that there are at least 900 publishing professional poets who turn out a book every two or four years; that in any month of the year in a typical medium-sized city at least 1,000 people have spent an evening listening to poetry being read—and yet, for a number of seemingly unalterable reasons, sales of a professional book of poems can be as small as two to five hundred copies?

In America the public is barraged by alternative cultural and entertainment attractions. Many people are not short of money to buy poetry books: they freely spend twenty or twenty-five dollars for best-seller fiction, murder mysteries, any kind of book they wish. They spend that sum on each video in their collection, each CD, for each opera, play, symphony, or ballet ticket. Not everyone likes to read, and not every reader enjoys poetry. There is no more reason to assume that someone who enjoys country-western will understand classical music, even though both are music, than that someone who enjoys romance novels, science fiction, how-to books, or even serious art fiction will understand and enjoy poetry simply because all are written in words. Unlike a manufacturer, the poet does not write to please the greatest number with his product—he has learned from and loved the poetry of past centuries, and he writes for the cumulatively large audience of centuries to come. *Increased publicity for* and *a real availability of* the books of American poets are urgent needs—a larger audience already exists for them if those two factors can change. Such an audience will make it possible for books to be printed and preserved. The NEA and the State Arts Councils might profitably work on that. *Helping to support reviews of books by poets, young and old, along with helping to subsidize shelves of poetry in bookstores seems to me a more urgent need for American poetry at present than making grants to individual poets.*

In the meantime, while we wait for Mr. Joseph Brodsky to turn all Americans into buyers and readers of good poetry, and while academics and critics like Denis Donaghue mourn the fact that American poetry can no longer be conveniently organized for the

Western mind into groups stemming from Eliot or Pound, or Stevens, so that it can be easily taught in the classroom and described in books of criticism, I have turned to the Eastern mind for my vision of the contemporary poetry scene. At the end of Forster's *A Passage to India* there is a religious celebration seen through the eyes of those who are not frightened by chaos and mystery. It is a scene of unanalyzable confusion, of mingled ugliness, beauty, and blur. At the riverbank, rockets are going off; some people are praising God without attributes; others see His attributes in this or that organ of the body or manifestation in the sky. "Above stood the secular power of Mau—elephants, artilleries, crowds . . . and singers struggled . . . preparing to throw God away, God himself (not that God can be thrown) into the storm. Thus was He thrown every year, and were others thrown—little images of Gampati, baskets of ten-day corn, tiny tazias after Mohurram-scapegoats, husks, emblems of passage; a passage not easy, not now, not here, not to be apprehended except when it was unattainable; the God to be thrown was an emblem of that. The village of Gokul reappeared on its tray . . . A servitor entered the dark waters pushing the village before him until the clay dolls slipped off their chairs and began to gutter in the rain, and King Kansa was confounded with the father and mother of the Lord . . . The oars, the sacred tray, the letters of Ronny and Adela, broke loose and floated confusedly. Artillery was fired, drums beaten, elephants trumpeted, and drowning all an immense peal of thunder . . . cracked like a mallet on the dome."

This, it seems to me, is an appropriate image for the confusion and profusion of American poetry, thrown into the river of readers and nonreaders as an offering to the gods of the human imagination, the gods of art and of language, the gods of the human spirit at its most innocent.

# Biographical Notes

## Beth Snow

For more than fifty years, Mona Van Duyn has written creative and critical works. She has published eight volumes of poetry as well as two short stories. In recognition of her skill and style, she has been awarded multiple accolades, among them the Pulitzer Prize and the appointment in 1992 as poet laureate of the United States.

A native Iowan, Mona Van Duyn was born in Waterloo, Iowa, on May 9, 1921, to Lora (nee Kramer) and Earl George Van Duyn, a gas station manager and later owner of a tobacco store and newsstand in Eldora, Iowa. Growing up in Eldora, Van Duyn was an avid reader of poetry and loved writing it although she received no support at home or at school. In an interview recorded in the autumn 1991 issue of *Iowa Woman* magazine, she recalls her parents admonishing her "to quit ruining her eyes and go out and play rather than read." Reading her way through the local public library (such as it was in a village of 3,200), she became a self-propelled poet who wrote privately and reveled in it. She recounts in the same article, "I had written secret notebooks all during grade school and high school, but I showed them to no one, neither parents nor children . . . In fact, [in grade school, learning] a poem was a punishment. One was made to stay after school and learn a poem. I loved this punishment" (20) (Van Duyn's insertion). Such an early glimpse of the poet is rare; this interview is an intriguing and provocative look at the usually reticent Van Duyn. Written by

Marianne Abel as part of a celebration of the two Iowa women who won Pulitzer Prizes in 1991, this piece allows insight into Van Duyn's professional life, marriage, and more private life.

In 1942, she obtained a B.A. degree from the University of Northern Iowa (formerly Iowa State Teachers College) where she wrote for the student magazine and was granted generous access to the otherwise closed campus stacks. It was there, too, that she began to admire the poetry of Rainier Maria Rilke, whose work she still enjoys. After graduation from U.N.I., she spent the summer working as a soda jerk in Evanston, Illinois, before moving on to the University of Iowa, which awarded her an M.A. in 1943. While working on her Ph.D. there, Van Duyn won the *Kenyon Review* Doubleday Doran Prize for an early short story; later, while teaching in Louisville, Kentucky, she was told by editors that, though they would love to have a novel by her, they could not publish a book of her stories because there was no market for short fiction. She decided to devote herself to poetry. In that same profile, she notes that, although the initial embrace of poetry was quick, much more time had to pass before she could recognize her role as poet: "I was always terrified of calling myself a poet: I always evaded it by saying, 'I write poetry.' I remember very well the first time I said, 'I am a poet,' you know, when people ask you what you do. It took two books before I said it. And since then, I claim to be a poet" (18).

Van Duyn married Jarvis A. Thurston (also a Ph.D. student at the University of Iowa) on August 31, 1943, and remained at the University of Iowa as a graduate student teacher and an English instructor during the years 1943 through 1946. From there, she and Thurston moved to Louisville, Kentucky, where they both took positions in the English department at the University of Louisville—she as an instructor, he as an assistant professor. They left in 1950. While in Louisville, she and Thurston founded the literary magazine *Perspective: A Quarterly of Literature* in 1947, supporting it from their own funds and editing it together until 1967. Poet W. S. Merwin, among others, was first published there.

After Louisville, the couple (and the magazine) moved to St. Louis, Missouri, where Thurston joined the full-time faculty and Van Duyn served as a lecturer in English in the University College at Washington University. Van Duyn enjoyed a long association with the University College adult education program until her retirement from teaching in 1990; she was also an adjunct professor in the English department in 1983, was named as the "Visiting Hurst Professor" in 1987, and acted as poetry consultant for the Modern Literature Collection of the school's Olin Library.

Although most of her formal teaching career was spent at Washington University, Van Duyn was actively involved in various writing workshops. Among her more notable positions were lecturer at the Salzburg Seminar in American Studies in Salzburg, Austria, in 1973; poet in residence at the Bread Loaf Writers' Conference for the years 1974 and 1976; and participant at the Sewanee Writing Conference in Tennessee in 1990 and 1991. She was the poetry advisor for the journal *College English* from 1955 to 1957. Van Duyn has published creative and critical works in a variety of magazines including *Atlantic,* the *Kenyon Review,* the *New Republic, Yale Review,* and the *New Yorker,* as well as contributing numerous reviews and poems to *Poetry* from 1944 to 1970.

Despite the amount of other work, poetry has always remained Van Duyn's primary career. In 1956, she won the Eunice Tietjens Memorial Prize from *Poetry* for her poem "Three Valentines to the Wide World," which appeared in her first book, *Valentines to the Wide World: Poems* (Cummington Press, 1959).

Her second volume, *A Time of Bees* (University of North Carolina Press), arrived in 1964. These poems draw upon a variety of metaphors from mental institutions to suburban gardening to an exploration of friendship to the dismantling of a beehive. This book generated mixed reviews encompassing the spectrum from mild admiration to a Helen Bullis Prize from *Poetry Northwest* in the same year.

From 1964 to 1971, Van Duyn's career took off; she received a grant from the National Endowment for the Arts for 1966 through 1967, the Harriet Monroe Memorial Prize given by *Poetry* in 1968, and, in the same year, the Hart Crane Memorial Award from American Weave Press. Six years after the publication of *A Time of Bees,* her third book, *To See, To Take* (Atheneum, 1970), provided Van Duyn with the Bollingen Prize in 1970 and the National Book Award in 1971.

In the early 1970s, the poet enjoyed other successes with a Guggenheim Fellowship for 1972 through 1973 and an honorary Litt.D. from Washington University in 1971 as well as one from Cornell College (Iowa) the following year. In this time, she published her fourth and fifth books. *Bedtime Stories* (Ceres Press, 1972) consists of pioneer narratives told in the voice of Van Duyn's grandmother, in a German-American dialect. *Merciful Disguises: Poems Published and Unpublished* (first issued from Atheneum in 1973 and reprinted in 1982) is a collection of poems from her previous books that also introduces a section entitled "Unpublished Poems 1965–1973." Closing out the decade, Van Duyn was honored with the 1976 Loines Prize given by the National Institute of Arts and Letters, which later granted her membership in 1987.

In 1981 she was named a fellow of the American Academy of Poets and in 1985 became one of its twelve chancellors. In 1982, she received the Sandburg Prize from Cornell College in Iowa. That same year her book *Letters from a Father and Other Poems* (Atheneum) was published; it chronicles the decline of her elderly parents, most poignantly in the popular title poem and in "The Stream," a well-received poem that describes the last days of her mother.

Van Duyn received another NEA grant in 1985; two years later the Poetry Society of America gave her its Shelley Memorial Award for her body of work, and two years after that the Modern Poetry Association named her the recipient of its Ruth Lilly Poetry Prize. She received the Pulitzer Prize for *Near Changes,* published in 1990 by Knopf. Also, in 1991 her alma mater, the University of Northern Iowa, presented Van Duyn with an honorary doctorate degree. She was appointed the U.S. Library of Congress Poet Laureate Consultant in Poetry for 1992 through 1993.

Prior to this honor, a little discussed booklet, *Lives and Deaths of the Poets and Non-Poets,* was privately published in 1991. Van Duyn's next collection arrived in 1993 from Knopf—*If It Be Not I: Collected Poems 1959–1982* was accompanied by the joint publication of *Firefall* (Knopf, 1993), a new volume of poetry.

Over the years, Van Duyn's poems have also been included in such collections as *Midland,* edited by Paul Engle and published by Random House in 1961; *The Honey and the Gall,* Chad Walsh, editor, published by Macmillan in 1967; the well-known feminist anthology *No More Masks!: An Anthology of Twentieth-Century American Women Poets,* Florence Howe, editor, which appeared in a revised form in 1993 by Harper Perennial; and the Annie Finch volume *A Formal Feeling Comes: Poems in Form by Contemporary Women* issued from Story Line Press in 1994.

# Contributors

Michael Bugeja is professor of journalism in the E. W. Scripps School of Journalism at Ohio University in Athens. *Talk,* a book of poems, is forthcoming from the University of Arkansas Press.

Sydney Burris is professor of English at the University of Arkansas at Fayetteville. He is the author of *A Day at the Races* (poems) and *The Poetry of Resistance,* a critical study of the poetry of Seamus Heaney.

Emily Grosholz is professor of philosophy at Pennsylvania State University. She is the author of *Eden* (poems) and the editor of *Telling the Barn Swallow: Poets on the Poetry of Maxine Kumin,* published in 1997 by the University of New England Press.

Rachel Hadas is professor of English at the Newark campus of Rutgers University and the author of many books of poetry, essays, and translations. Her most recent publications are *The Double Legacy,* memoirs published by Faber & Faber; and *The Empty Bed,* a book of poems.

Jane Hoogestraat is associate professor of English at Southwest Missouri State University. She has published poems in *Poetry* and *Southern Review* and critical essays on the poetry of Ezra Pound, Adrienne Rich, and Susan Howe.

Richard Howard, who teaches at Columbia University, won the Pulitzer Prize for Poetry in 1970 for *Untitled Subjects.* His critical study *Alone with America: Essays on the Art of Poetry in the United*

*States* was reissued in 1980. His most recent book of poems is *Like Most Revelations.*

Carolyn Kizer won the Pulitzer Prize for Poetry in 1985 for *YIN: New Poems.* The author of eight books of poetry, she published *Harping On* in 1996.

Maxine Kumin was awarded the Pulitzer Prize for Poetry in 1973. Her new books are *Looking for Luck, Connecting the Dots,* and *Selected Poems 1960–1990,* all from Norton.

Wyatt Prunty directs the Sewanee Writers Conference. His most recent books are *Since the Noon Mail Stopped* and *The Run of the House* (poems), and *Fallen from the Symboled World: Precedents for the New Formalism.*

Beth Snow holds an M.A. in English from Southwest Missouri State University. She plans to enter the workforce for a time before pursuing her terminal degree.

Ann Townsend teaches at Denison University. She won the Gerald Cable Prize for *Dime Store Erotics* (Silverfish Review Press, 1997).

Stephen Yenser, professor of English at the University of California at Los Angeles, is the author of *The Fire in All Things* (poems) and *The Consuming Myth: The Work of James Merrill.*